LONDON TRANSPORT

BUSES & COACHES

1956

LONDON TRANSPORT
BUSES & COACHES

1956

Including a supplement of
photographs covering the years
1939-45 and 1948-55

John A.S. Hambley

Published in 1997 by
Harold Martin & Redman Ltd

in conjunction with JOHN A.S. HAMBLEY
7 Linden Road,
Dunstable,
Beds. LU5 4NZ

Additional text and research by David A. Ruddom

British Library Cataloguing in Publication Data
A catalogue record for this book is available from the British Library

ISBN 1 901394 04 2

Front cover photograph:
On 6th June only days after having been returned to service from its first overhaul, shining RT3712 is pictured at Mitcham with the image of a car about to pass by reflecting on its lower panels. The bus, which now carries an RT3 body, is in use as AL11 on Route 152 and is destined for "Hook, Ace of Spades ONLY". The use of the word 'only' for short workings ceased some years before but obviously Merton garage took care of their blinds and made them last. (W.R.Legg)

Back cover photograph:
The final operational garage for RT1493 was Leyton and the bus is seen here in use on Route 10 heading through the East End bound for Victoria along a roadway surfaced with granite setts. A Morris car follows at a safe distance while, travelling in the opposite direction, the pillion passenger on the motorcycle nonchalantly rests his arm on the roof of the attached sidecar. Later in the year under review this RT would be dispatched to Bird's Commercial Motors for immediate resale to Cunningham's Bus Service of Paisley to give a further seven years service in its new surroundings. (A.M.Wright)

Designed and produced by Harold Martin & Redman Ltd.
Printed and bound in Great Britain.

Standing at the bus stop on Putney Hill, having negotiated the cross roads at Upper Richmond Road, RTL34 has not much further to travel before reaching its destination of the Green Man on the edge of Putney Heath. Presumably it is waiting for a new crew to take up duties and it is possible they have thumbed a lift on the RT coming up behind which is on Route 93, the route which shares this bus stop. The RTL had entered service in January 1949 from West Green garage and it was transferred to Chelverton Road, Putney in March 1956. After a short stay and a brief spell at Riverside it moved on to Walworth where it was to spend around two years before being disposed of to Bird's Commercial Motors, the Stratford-upon-Avon dealer. (W.R.Legg)

Acknowledgements

Without the kindness and expert knowledge of the many photographers and owners of collections of London Transport photographs this book could not have been produced. I should like to especially thank the following: Norman Anscomb, James H.Aston, R.K.Blencowe, C.Carter, Alan B.Cross, John Gascoine, J.C.Gillham, Peter Gomm, Peter Gulland, W.J.Haynes, Roy Hobbs, Laurie Housden, Fred Ivey, D.A. Jones, D.W.K.Jones, Kevin Lane, Mrs B.Legg, John Lines, Michael Lockyer, London Trolleybus Preservation Society, I.Maclean, Roy Marshall, B.Montgomery G.R.Mortimer, National Tramways Museum, A.G.Newman, A.D.Packer, John G.E.Nye, B.Rackman, Norman Rayfield, Geoff Rixon, Mike Rooum, D.Trevor Rowe, Lyndon Rowe, David A.Ruddom, P.F.Sapte, R.H.G.Simpson, John G.S.Smith, Peter Snell, Brian Speller, Ray Stanmore, The Omnibus Society, Sheila Taylor of the London Transport Museum, Ron Wellings and A.M.Wright.

All the uncredited photographs are from the author's collection, which has been built up over many years. I would be very pleased to hear from any photographer not credited who identifies his work so that due acknowledgement can be made in a future book of this series.

The factual information on which the picture captions are based has come from many published sources and individual specialists. In particular grateful acknowledgement is made to the London Historical Research Group of the Omnibus Society, the London Omnibus Traction Society, the P.S.V.Circle, Peter Gomm of the RT/RF Register, David A.Ruddom and John G.S.Smith.

On a more personal note, a warm hearted thank you is extended to my wife Iris and David Ruddom's wife Enid who have kept both of us supplied with refreshment and have unselfishly shown great patience and forbearance in our long hours of deliberation.

Publisher's Note

The photographic supplement to previous books in the series contained in the 1946 volume was received with considerable acclaim. It is intended therefore to incorporate a similar section in future books as opportunity occurs in order to make use of some fascinating material received relevant to years already published. Previously unpublished photographs are continually coming to light and if you have such items which would benefit from a wider audience then please do get in touch with the author whose address is to be found on the back of the title page.

Two printed listings of all the vehicles shown in this series of books are available, one in fleet number order and the other in route number order. Each list gives fleet number, registration number, route or service engaged on, location, source of photograph with year and page number of the book in which it is published. These are only available direct from the author at Dunstable and are priced at £5.00 each. Please state whether you require fleet number or route number order when ordering.

Introduction

1956 continued the downward trend in the fortunes of London Transport experienced in the previous year. True the drop in number of passengers carried was not as considerable as in 1955 but nevertheless it was still on the slippery slope. At the end of the year the Suez crisis was to lead to a 'Catch 22' situation whereby fuel rationing was imposed which meant a sudden increased demand for public transport which London Transport was well equipped to meet, having a sizeable reserve fleet of vehicles available. However, LT itself was required to achieve a 5% reduction in fuel consumption and so the opportunity to impress the beleagured private car users was stunted by the service reductions necessary and eventually by the increase in the minimum fare from 2d to 3d at the turn of the year.

There were many aspects of transport life in London which were changing in 1956. The granite road setts and wooden tar blocks on the road surfaces were being replaced by smoother tarmacadam finishes which gave for more comfortable travel. The introduction of clean air measures were beginning to ease the incidence of the famous London 'pea-souper' fogs which disrupted services so badly. Transport employees were realizing the benefits of a shorter working week which was introduced in stages during 1956 as part of the pay settlement agreed in the previous year. Methods of fare collection were being modernised and Gibson and Setright Speed ticket machines were further introduced to the detriment of the Bell Punch tickets we all loved to collect. By the end of the year machines were in use at fifty garages and the Green Line operation had been totally converted.

No new garages opened during 1956 but the vast Aldenham Bus Overhaul works was officially opened and the new garage and bus station at Hounslow was completed. In the Country Area the extension of the garage at Grays was commissioned and right at the beginning of the year the new bus station - really only a lay by off Waterhouse Street - was opened at Hemel Hempstead.

Staying with the Country Area, route developments continued in the various new town areas and in May another of the perpetual shake-ups of the network of services around Grays took place. 1956 marked the first major conversions to one man operation using the larger sized RFs. Among the earliest routes were 308/A, 317/A, 384/A and 399. At the same time in July a new Green Line route was commenced using the unoccupied 719 number and introducing coach operation to Garston garage. This route ran between Hemel Hempstead and Victoria via Watford, Stanmore, Kingsbury and Willesden and was said to be provided to make it easier for family links to be maintained between new town residents and their former homes - something the new town administrators were believed to discourage! It was ironic that the number 719 should have been brought into use at this time since it had originally been intended for a Green Line route which never materialised from Windsor to Luton via Uxbridge, Watford and St.Albans. Four months earlier in March much of this road had been covered not by a Green Line route but by a new Express Country Area bus route 803 from Uxbridge to Welwyn Garden City.

In the Central Area route changes in the main amounted to tinkering in order to meet economies of operation and declining passenger usage. There were localisation exercises like the 270 introduced between Kensington and Teddington, odd extensions to serve developing areas like 103 which went north from Eastern Avenue, Pettits Lane to Chase Cross and quite a few Sunday curtailments such as 94 between Lewisham and Brockley Rise and 168 between Vauxhall and Horse Guards Avenue. Bus services which had replaced the rigid tram routes began to be integrated more fully into the bus network, a good example being 176 which usurped the long standing association of Route 1 with the road to Willesden on weekdays. One very old route number, the 32, which by this time was only a tiny shadow of its former self, finally disappeared in the October changes.

While this series of books does not deal with trolleybuses, this form of transport experienced the biggest drop in passenger use during the year. As if to reflect the impending doom, in October the 683 route lost its off-peak and Saturday service and the peak hour 565 service between Barking and Holborn Circus disappeared altogether.

Changes to the operating fleet resulted in a further drop in the total number of buses and coaches owned. The only new vehicles to enter passenger service during the year were RM1 and six RTs (4787-4792) but these have already been included in the stock figures of previous years. RM1's entry into service was of course a great event and for the first time the public could experience the distinctive rumble of an AEC Routemaster engine and the maroon decor of the interior. It was allocated to Cricklewood and rostered for duties which involved it in mileage in excess of 1,000 miles per week. The RTs were brought out of store at Loughton garage.

Thirty STL class vehicles were disposed of during the year but these had been withdrawn from passenger service in earlier years. All 120 Craven bodied RTs were now withdrawn from service and by the end of the year 95 had been disposed of to Bird's at Stratford upon Avon. A further 32 T class vehicles were disposed of and this figure was made up of those withdrawn during the year and earlier. Eight of the TD class were withdrawn in 1956, seven of which were disposed of by the year end. The net result of all this was that London Transport owned 164 fewer buses and coaches at the end of the year than at the beginning.

The celebration of the year as far as the transport enthusiast was concerned was the centenary of the formation of the London General Omnibus Company in 1856. This was marked by events in the London Bus Week held between 16th and 21st July - not a specifically accurate date as far as the LGOC was concerned but aimed at high summer and optimum weather and crowd conditions. A parade was held in Regents Park on the 16th and the week ended with a line up of historic vehicles on Horse Guards Parade on Saturday 21st July. It has to be remembered that in 1956 these vehicles were secreted away at Reigate garage and so their appearance caused considerable excitement. A four week long exhibition was staged in the booking hall of Charing Cross (now Embankment) Underground Station and London Transport published the paperback book "London General", which nowadays fetches a good price if offered at transport flea markets.

Victoria garage had a Sundays only allocation on Route 24 from 1952 to 1958 and on 12th August RT3343 passes some high rise dwellings in Pimlico. The tall flats have an air of newness as yet not disfigured by vandalism and graffiti and represent the new age of optimism. The social problems of such blocks were yet to be discovered. (W.R.Legg)

In January sunshine green RT79 exits from Hertford Bus Station, also known as Hertford Car Park, into Maidenhead Street with the Evergreen Club Hall in the background. Throughout 1956 these 2RT2s were the vehicles allocated to Route 327 since they met the weight restriction imposed on the bridge at Broxbourne. Eventually bridge renovation meant they were relegated to more mundane uses as learners and staff buses but for the moment their distinctive engine tones could be enjoyed in the County town and its surroundings. (D.W.K.Jones)

Originally Rye Lane garaged but now operated by Sidcup after receiving its first overhaul, dusty RT2774 is in use on the circular Route 132 at Eltham, Well Hall Station. Interestingly only a careful study of the route blind indicates which way round the loop at Bexleyheath and Bexley the bus is operating – in this case clockwise. There are no yellow blinds or qualified destinations but presumably the local users managed to differentiate their buses. (W.R.Legg)

Cullings Coaches of Claxton, Norfolk were the owners of ex-STD96 from July 1955 and the bus now stands outside the operator's head office with an interesting route blind reading "BERGH – APTON AND DISTRICT SERVICES". Both named villages stand astride the main A146 halfway between Norwich and Beccles. The loss of the roof mounted route number box has altered the appearance of the bus considerably but the addition of a driver's cab door was doubtless welcomed by the Norfolk drivers. (Roy Marshall)

Passing through Croydon on 13th September, recently overhauled RT3694 looks immaculate although the author of this book has an aversion to the red oxide painted wheel trims. Emerging from its first overhaul in June carrying body number 2108 which was originally mounted on RT829, the vehicle spent a month at Sutton garage before reallocation to Elmers End. It remained here until its next overhaul in January 1960. (W.R.Legg)

RTL592 stands at Bromley by Bow about to depart for Eltham, Southend Crescent on Route 108A while, in the background, an RF with blinds set for Route 208 to Clapton Pond continues its rest period. Originally a through service from Clapton Pond to various South London termini was operated but the section between Clapton and Bromley by Bow was separated in 1927 when double deck NS buses to a special design were introduced. The low bridge in Kenworthy Road was the reason for this split and the northern single deck section, first numbered 108D, became 208 in 1934. The 108A route seen here was a 1944 introduction to serve the Rochester Way area. (R.H.G.Simpson)

Red liveried RT1500 has been retrieved from the interior of Stockwell garage and made ready for its transfer to the Country Area, having spent some six months in store. The move to Windsor garage earned it a repaint into Lincoln green livery only for it to be put back into store later in the year, this time at Shepherds Bush before eventual disposal in April 1957. (LT Museum U58493)

Egham, rather than the more logical Staines, was where London Transport met Aldershot & District and RT2317 stands at Egham Station in September with miscellaneous railway trucks and Aldershot & District Guy Arab 893 to keep it company. The via blind of the RT is interesting being unusually skimpy on detail while that carried by the Aldershot Guy goes over the top on information at the expense of clarity. (N.N.Forbes/National Tramway Museum)

This is the RT with a snout. Careful inspection of the bonnet of RT3326 will reveal an insert added at the front end which extended the radiator forward by two to three inches. This bus had entered service in October 1951 from Palmers Green garage and after receiving its first overhaul was fitted with a supercharger by Wellworthys at Lymington in December 1955. The extension was to accommodate this equipment. The bus entered service at Turnham Green, home of many experiments due to its proximity to Chiswick Works, in January 1956. Alas the experiment did not prove successful and although the RT was to keep its unique appearance until its next overhaul in September 1959, the supercharger had in fact been disconnected only a few months after fitment. Here the bus waits at Ealing to return home on a garage journey which will not fulfil the promise of the slip board. (A.B.Cross)

RT882 passes through Woolwich on its way to Camden Town while operating as AM18 on Route 53 on 7th September. Many years later after further body changes and following its disposal by the LTE, this RT had the distinction of being stolen and was presumably broken up for spares as it has never been seen since. (W.R.Legg)

Old Kent Road garage's RT3396 was originally delivered with a Weymann RT8 body but following its January overhaul is now fitted with an early RT3 type and is pictured at the Lewisham terminus of Route 89A. This route had been introduced in January 1955 between Lewisham and Woolwich, being an extension of the short lived 256 from Woolwich to Shooters Hill through the hilly Woodlands Estate and it provided a service through to Lewisham over the roads used by long standing Route 89. The badly wound blind does not show the crucial 'Eglinton Hill' line. (W.R.Legg)

RT2571 en-route for Kingston by way of Route 85 passes through the trees of Putney Heath soon to break out in summer foliage on 7th April. One boy wears long trousers while the other two wear the more customary short variety of the period. The 85 route has experienced a remarkably long untroubled existence commencing on 3rd August 1912 between Putney Bridge and Roehampton with a Sunday extension to the Kingston Hill tram terminus. It first reached Kingston town centre in January 1914. Apart from Sunday extensions to Leatherhead, Guildford and Dorking in the twenties it has remained faithful to its well worn path. (W.R.Legg)

Camberwell garaged RTL50 at Old Town, Clapham Common on 15th September has its destination blind set in readiness for a journey to Chingford Hatch on Route 35. This route originated with the Great Eastern London Motor Omnibus Company and was taken over by the LGOC in 1911 since when it has continued a north east to south west link across London Bridge, albeit now only reaching north as far as Shoreditch. (W.R.Legg)

What was once STL1158 looks in a very sad condition in September dumped on the land which S.Blackwell and Sons of Earls Colne, Essex reserved for vehicles which could be said to be past their prime. Having been withdrawn from service by LTE in June 1950 the bus then passed to Daniels the dealer of Rainham ostensibly for scrap but presumably it was acquired by Blackwells for spares as it was never operated. Eventually it was used as a paint store and in the early sixties it was cut down to single deck condition after it had partially collapsed. (B.Rackman)

RTL920 travels along Queen Victoria Street with half the familiar frontage to the Royal Exchange visible in the distance. Also included in the scene is a uniformed gentleman who is either a commissionaire or a bank messenger, several city gents and some sightseers strolling in the warm weather. An AEC lorry follows this Leyland interloper which has replaced the buses of that make so long associated with Putney Bridge garage from which it is working. Alas, two years later both the garage and the route would also disappear from the London scene in the cutbacks following the disastrous strike of 1958. (C.Carter)

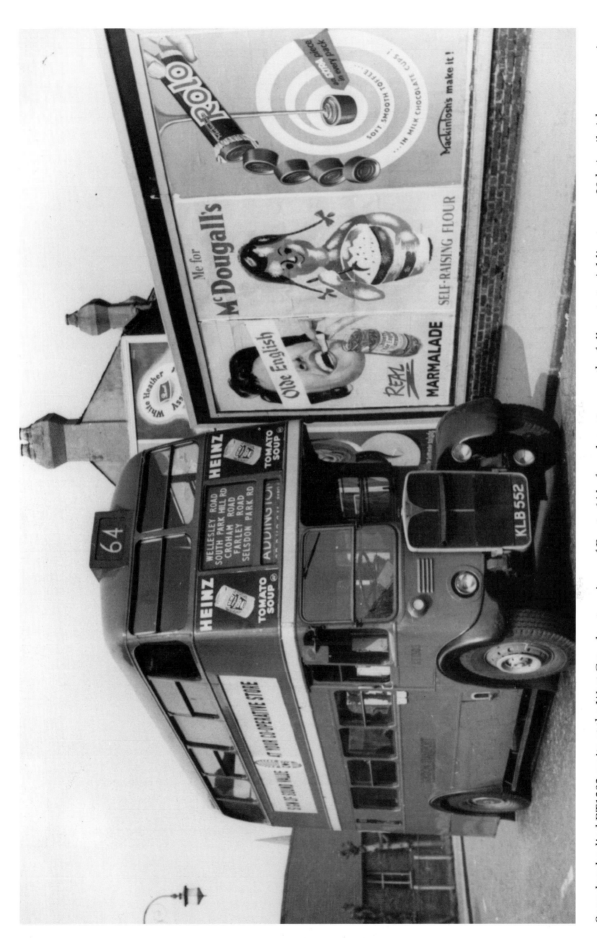

Saunders bodied RT1303 waits at the West Croydon terminus of Route 64 before departure on the full route to Addington on 20th April. A heavy pruning exercise has been carried out on the trees in the background but come summer they will have sprouted again with new growth. In a couple of years they will be back to the view which appears on page 87 of the 1954 book of this series. Check out that picture too for some of the advertising on the hoarding which, although different, is still dominated by the same manufacturers. (W.R.Legg)

Seen at Haven Green, Ealing on 10th April, Southall garaged T755 is about to depart for the Red Lion at Greenford. These post-war examples of the T class were not initially allocated to Southall when new but arrived in January 1953 for Route 211 replacing slightly newer TDs. With the large programme of route changes and service reductions in the months following the seven week long bus strike in 1958, surplus RFs became available to finally oust this batch of fifty Weymann bodied buses from the fleet. (J.C.Gillham)

No attempt has been made to remove the distinctive exterior ventilator scoops carried on this Park Royal body numbered in the London Transport series 6350. It had been thought necessary to fit RT2776 with additional ventilation equipment which was housed in the bulkheads for the vehicle's role as the 'rides' bus of the trio which toured America in 1952. Careful inspection reveals that the semaphore type trafficator arm is still in place but probably out of use by now. Here it stands at Gants Hill having turned short on the Eastern Avenue route 66. Upon its various visits to works for overhaul the body always emerged carrying its original fleet number until its final visit in January 1969 when it was outshopped as RT1708. (C.Carter)

Red liveried RT1490 passes through Watford on its journey from Mill Way Estate to Croxley Green, Manor Way by way of route 385. On loan to Watford High Street garage it was then transferred to Windsor before, in May, it received Country Area livery, as did a number of Craven bodied RTs between March and May. One year after receiving its new colours this fine looking vehicle was sold to Bird's Commercial Motors of Stratford-upon-Avon to eventually find further use north of the border. The Maypole grocers reminds one of an age before the supermarkets and if you look carefully their errand boy's bike is resting against the kerb ready to deliver your order. (A.B.Cross)

With the well known circular structure of the booking hall of Arnos Grove Underground Station on the Piccadilly Line as a background, TD17 waits to take up a further journey to Burnt Oak, Edgware Road as duty MH2 on Route 251. The minimum fare slip board applies to journeys at the western end of the route. Only a handful of their original complete batch of thirty one 1TD1s remained at Muswell Hill garage in 1956 and the 251 route was where they were usually to be found. (C.Carter)

Partially shaded by the well established trees on the edge of Putney Common, RT1809 with an RTW parked close behind, waits for departure time before commencing a journey to Redbridge Station on Route 96. As it transpired this RT was to reside at Forest Gate garage from its entry into service in July 1950 until its second overhaul in August 1958 after which it re-entered service from Potters Bar.

(John A.S.Hambley)

Nearly four years old now, RT3584 is graced with a set of 'lazy' route blinds which were most suitable for the short Route 251A which operated in peak hours between Arnos Grove Station and North Finchley. The bus is climbing Oakleigh Road and following in the distance is a roofbox RT on the much longer 84 route to St.Albans. In the first stage of the Central Area cutbacks which took place on the 20th August this route 251A would be withdrawn completely. (D.A.Ruddom collection)

An atmospheric view within the long defunct West Green garage shows a line up of parked RTL class vehicles. The garage was the original home of A.T.Bennett's famous Admiral fleet of independent buses which would have presented a very different profile. RTL995 is nearest the camera with the old style five line intermediate point blind for Route 29 while RTL1246 standing next to it displays the newer four line intermediate point blind for Route 231. The same mixture of older and newer via point blinds are fitted to the other unidentifiable vehicles.

Resting in Charlmont Road near to Tooting Broadway on Sunday only Route 77B, Camberwell garaged RTL689 will use Vauxhall rather than Lambeth Bridge to reach its northerly destination of Euston thereby providing a service to the Tate Gallery as emphasised by the slip board. Merton and Walworth garages had previously operated this route but on 2nd May Camberwell took over the Walworth duties. This bus was a long time resident of Camberwell garage whose public service vehicles were exclusively RTL for many years. (J.Gascoine collection)

The new docking and maintenance area of the rebuilt Hounslow garage on 9th October highlights the very high standard of the facilities provided by London Transport in ensuring that its vehicles were kept in a roadworthy condition. RT3585 sits comfortably over a maintenance pit which has had the connecting bridge tidily put to one side while RT4399 waits to be placed over the well lit and airy pit nearest the camera. Various other RTs are parked in the spacious building which could accommodate 110 similar sized vehicles if needed. (LT Museum 17492)

RT3593 stands at the Chipstead Valley terminus of Route 166 sometime in October before returning to Thornton Heath High Street. This route had come into existence on 7th April 1948 when the weekday operation of Route 59 was renumbered. The bus, having been returned to service after its initial overhaul received in March, is operated by Croydon garage. The sturdy wooden shelter is redolent of outer suburbia. (A.B.Cross)

The limited stop service 472 from Leatherhead to Netherne Hospital south of Coulsdon was introduced in April 1953, initially on Sundays only but later a Wednesday journey was added. Here at the Carshalton Road, Sutton bus stop RT1081 is about to depart, continuing its journey to this isolated hospital. At this stage the service fulfilled a very definite need judging by the well laden bus. (D.A.Ruddom collection)

In March RTL9 received its second overhaul and emerged from works carrying this roof box body number 2065 originally mounted on RT795. Previously only the prototype RTL501 had carried this style of body. A further roof box RTL was to follow in May when RTL36 received its overhaul. All three examples were disposed of to Bird's of Stratford upon Avon in 1958 and London was without this type of oddity until more examples appeared in 1964. The bus is seen in Netherfields Road, just off Tooting Bec Road, on 28th April in between journeys on Route 19 and operating from Battersea garage. (W.R.Legg)

Standing in Liverpool Street outside Broad Street Station, RTW384 with duty plates D28 has had its destination blind set for its journey to Shepherds Bush, Wells Road. These eight feet wide all Leyland products were a familiar sight on this route for many years having replaced 7'6" wide vehicles on 11th April 1951 as part of the second major reallocation of the type after the successful trials in Central London. (Photomatic Ltd.)

Waiting at the deserted Becontree Heath terminus of Route 23, situated just off Wood Lane, RTL655 looks as if it has been abandoned as it waits for some form of human contact. Despite the impressive list of places served on the blind, its next journey will only be as far as Barking Broadway, a destination display not so commonly seen as other Barking termini. Metro-Cammell only built 450 bodies for the RT family of buses and they were placed on the chassis of RTL551 through to RTL1000. Not being interchangeable with other manufacturer's products their life always revolved around this series of fleet numbers. (M.Rooum)

RT110 now demoted to learner duties carries the body number 341 now with a replacement roof route number box. Not unusual you might say but this is the bus which for many years was the odd man out among the 2RT2s by not having such a fitment, having lost it during the war years. The exact dates of the loss and refitment have not been established but any information on this would be most welcome.

An ex-London 4STD3 finds itself parked in Mostar, Yugoslavia, with the Dinaric Alps rising in the background. The registration number now carried, 6X3125, unfortunately at the present time does not give any clue as to the previous identity of the bus. No use has been made of the blind boxes and a simple slip board suffices to carry one piece of route information in the lower saloon front window above the bonnet. The front dome has taken some knocks from overhanging trees since the exile of this all Leyland product. (D.Trevor Rowe)

New Express Route 803 operating between Welwyn Garden City Station and Uxbridge Station was introduced on 21st March serviced by six RTs from Garston garage. Here RT4547 stands at the Uxbridge terminus displaying its white on blue blinds before departing for its easterly destination on the full route which operated in peak hours and Saturdays only. Off peak on Monday to Friday the service only operated between St.Albans and Rickmansworth. The six buses needed for the service were available since the number of vehicles on Route 351 were reduced by a similar amount. (C.Carter)

On Sunday 11th November Grays garaged RT3178 performs on a Railway Emergency Service caused by engineering work between Purfleet and Grays. In addition to the bus it appears that a railway van has been provided to deal with any unwieldy luggage. Two railmen wait to deal with any large trunks which might have been accompanying passengers making for Tilbury (Riverside) and the docks. (F.Church)

On 27th June the Central Road Services Department made a number of route changes, among them being alterations to Routes 1, 60 and 176. New route 260 was also introduced running on its fullest journeys between Colindale and Surrey Docks and was in reality short workings of Route 60 extended and diverted to cover part of Route 1. RT395 on duty W2 stands in the apparently empty bus stand at Cornwall Road, Waterloo ready to return to Cricklewood Garage. Nowadays this is the site of the Red Arrow garage. (J.Gascoine collection)

Various members of the pre-war class of 10T10 coaches were still in evidence during the year and three can be seen within the perimeter of Reigate garage. From left to right T621, T613 and T631 stand on the sloping ground by the garage entrance. The date is 8th April and all three vehicles are engaged in staff transport duties between the Surrey headquarters of the Country Area and Chiswick Works in West London. (Roy Hobbs)

First entering passenger service with LPTB in June 1937 ex-STD78 has been used to provide living accommodation for members of the Hamsters Operatic Society theatre group based in East Ham when on tour. The bus was affectionately named 'Hambuster' and is seen here at Bow Bridge in March with advertising from an earlier tour to the West Country to perform 'An Italian Straw Hat' in aid of the British Empire Cancer Campaign. The hamster on the side carries a collecting box, a more worthy occupation than the badger of recent years who merely sniffed at rear wheels. Eventually the bus became a target for vandals and being damaged beyond repair was sold in August 1962 to be replaced by another ex-London Transport vehicle in the shape of RT89. (P.Gulland)

The 394 set of routes served the many hamlets in the hilly area of Buckinghamshire between Chesham and Great Missenden on the extremity of the London Transport Northern Country Area. RF686 with driver/conductor already seated in his cab is about to take up duties on the 394B variant to Great Missenden Station from Chesham (Nashleigh Arms). This RF, having been converted to OMO operation in July was quickly moved into Amersham garage for the introduction of this mode of operation on this group of routes which took place on the 11th of that month. (P.Gomm collection).

The chassis of ex-London Transport B4, now carrying its third body, is seen in Delamere Street, Chester on 21st April. Originally delivered with a Park Royal highbridge 56 seat body in May 1942, the bus was always operated by Hanwell garage in its LT days. Disposed of to Crosville Motor Services in January 1953 it received the second hand lowbridge Strachan body once carried by MB187 (FFM343) before entering service. In February 1956 the third body as shown here was fitted. It is an ECW example built in 1949 and was once carried by M40 (FM6416). The Crosville fleet number MB163 was carried until May 1958 when a renumbering exercise gave the bus the number DKA163. (J.G.E.Nye)

RM1 proudly proclaims 'This is the Routemaster, London's Bus of the Future' as it departs along Horse Guards Road from the Centenary Exhibition on 21st July. Who could have realised then that forty years later a substantial number of the class in various liveries and configurations would still be in operation serving the needs of the travelling public in London and elsewhere. (G.R.Mortimer)

Recently overhauled RTL171, soon to depart from Liverpool Street Station on Route 7 to Acton High Street, carries the latest LTE innovation of all over one colour wheel trims. This bus operated at Sidcup garage from new in March 1949 until transferred to Middle Row in the early months of 1955. It was withdrawn from service in October 1958, moved to store at Willesden in November and disposed of to the Ceylon Transport Board along with sixty two other members of the class in the month of December. (Photomatic Ltd.)

RF289 entered service as a 41 seat Central Area 2RF2 bus in September 1952 from Muswell Hill garage. With the need for additional coaches in 1956, RF289 to RF294 were repainted into Green Line livery, passenger saloon doors and luggage racks were fitted together with side route board brackets and the vehicles reclassified 2RF2/3. Subsequently at the end of the year work was carried out to reseat them to carry 40 passengers. Immediately after its transformation in March RF289 was based at Victoria garage as the substitute emergency coach where it stands awaiting its call to duty with an RFW coach parked closely behind. Note the abbreviated blind display which enabled all Green Line routes to be contained on the roller blind and the side route board which merely says "Green Line" with provision for the appropriate route numbers to be slotted over the ends, in this case 709. (A.B.Cross)

Friday Hill East at Chingford Hatch provides the stand for RT3371 while it takes a rest from working on Route 191 out of Enfield garage. Further along the road a roof box RT can be seen turning on Route 35. Route 191 replaced the additional service on 102 between Edmonton and Chingford Hatch on 6th October 1954 and the extension beyond Lower Edmonton Station to Bounces Road, which is the next destination of this bus, only operated on weekdays. (W.R.Legg)

RTL737 in admirable weather conditions passes over Westminster Bridge with County Hall as a backdrop. The foundation stone to the first building which made up this headquarters of the now defunct London County, later Greater London, Council was laid in 1912. When the various additions were finally completed in 1963 County Hall employed 7,000 people but nowadays it lies empty amid so much controversy over its future use – how times change! Route 176 came into existence with the fifth stage of the tram to bus conversion programme on 7th October 1951 operating between Catford and the Embankment, Horse Guards Avenue. Here it is seen at the end of its tram replacement format, since on 27th June it would cross the Thames by Waterloo rather than Westminster Bridge and continue over the erstwhile Route 1 to Willesden Garage. Today it has lost its north west London section but still runs through the points shown here on the intermediate blind but in a two-tone green livery. (F.W.Ivey)

Ex-London Transport D111, now Belfast Corporation 480, is at the point of having its original Brush built body removed prior to receiving a new highbridge body built by Harkness. The date is 8th February and the location Bog Meadows in Belfast, which was only a short walk from the Belfast Corporation Falls Road depot. (B.Montgomery)

In 1956, Mr.J.B.Burnell, Operating Manager of Central Road Services of LTE, was President of the Omnibus Society and on the Sunday following the Annual Dinner he arranged a special tour using two RTs, 913 and 2775. The trip on 23rd September started on Victoria Embankment, crossed the Thames at Tower Bridge, Rotherhithe Tunnel and, most spectacularly, on the Woolwich Free Ferry. In midstream the RTs are carried to the opposite bank of the river aboard one of the two rather ageing boats which provided this service in 1956. (Roy Marshall)

In 1948/49 a batch of twelve STLs were converted into tower wagons for dealing with the overhead equipment of the tram and trolleybus system, mainly replacing a group of similar vehicles based on ADC or old NS chassis which dated from the 1930s. This is 726J which used the chassis of former STL314. Painted all over red, it is allocated to the Electrical Equipment Engineer at Manor House and in this picture appears to have strayed away from the overhead wires it is supposed to look after. It was eventually withdrawn in May 1960 and sold to W.North of Leeds. (R.Stanmore)

RF684 was converted for one man operation and reclassified 2RF5/1 in February and, just visible at the top of the nearside windscreen, a sticker commands "Pay As You Enter, Fares Ready Please". Perhaps it is just as well this is rather indistinct since the 307 route on which the bus operates remained crew operated until October 1957. The bus is seen in the Hemel Hempstead bus station, which was brought into use the previous month. A nice looking Bedford OB of Rover Bus Services rests alongside to complete the picture. (R.H.G.Simpson)

The two RTs used for the special tour of the Omnibus Society on 23rd September continued after their crossing on the Woolwich Free Ferry to visit Charlton Works, Reigate Garage (where lunch was enjoyed in a marquee), Chessington Zoo and Stockwell Garage. In particular those taking part viewed the museum items at these various locations. In this view RTs 2775 and 913 are joined at Charlton Works by RT105, the Plumstead garage staff bus. Slip boards mounted above the bonnets proclaim 'The Omnibus Society, London'. (R.H.G.Simpson)

This was once B23 in the London fleet and is now MB194 of Crosville Motor Service Ltd., albeit with a 1948 built ECW body. This body, maker's number 3105 of Series 2, had previously been mounted since new on a 1932 AEC Regent which Crosville had first had on hire in December 1945 from Brighton, Hove and District Omnibus Company and then later purchased. In 1954 the AEC chassis was disposed of for scrap and in November the body reappeared on this ex-London Bristol K6A chassis, the combination staying together until scrapped in October 1965. A nice selection of other vehicles keep company with the subject of the camera.

A study in rear ends (of the buses not the people!) finds GS12 and RT128 in the bleak but practical surroundings of Hertford Bus Station. Both vehicles are excellent testimonies to the body designer's art, the GS coming from Eastern Coach Works while the staff of LPTB evolved the RT. The bicycle with its metal chain guard is a period piece in itself. (D.W.K.Jones)

The familiar shape of the grandstand at Epsom racecourse is seen in the far distance as 420W stands on the higher ground at the Tattenham Corner end of this part of the Downs. As is usual with race meetings here, the skyline is filled with all forms of road transport. The chassis for this 6 ton towing lorry is that of ex-T159 earmarked for its new role in November 1939. First appearing in this form in February 1940 it was to complete twenty one year's further service. Previously it had only managed nine years in use as a 27 seat rear entrance Green Line coach, having entered service in September 1930 operating out of Watford, Leavesden Road garage.

The London Gun Club of Northolt used ex-STL1590 for storage purposes for a short period in the mid 1950s. An obvious requirement was the immediate fitment of a secure door to the rear platform area of the STL11 type body and apart from an additional window added to the lower rear one, nothing else would appear to have been materially changed. The club's name has been prominently added and one cannot help but reflect that forty years later this would be totally inappropriate and an obvious target for graffiti artists, vandals and would-be thieves. (N.Rayfield)

With the fine looking Clarendon Hotel at Watford Junction Station behind and the Malden Hotel to the left of the picture, RT3732 passes by with badly positioned route blinds but definitely en-route to Croxley Green, Manor Way by way of Route 385. Before Garston garage opened, this route was the responsibility of Leavesden Road (WT) but when that closed it passed to Watford High Street (WA) rather than the new Garston. In 1956 however GR did supply two additional RTs on weekdays. Carrying duty plates WA48, this RT had been transferred to Watford High Street in July 1953 together with a small number of other members of the class previously operating out of Guildford. (R.Stanmore)

The only part of this view at Uxbridge Station which is recognisable today is the sloping glass windows of the Underground Station which are now incorporated into the new bus station facilities. Behind where Windsor's RT1517 is standing is now part of the present day Uxbridge garage of Centrewest. Routes 457 and 457A were the main service from here to Slough and Windsor in 1956, the 457A variant deviating on its approach to Slough via Upton Lea. Nowadays no bus route at all serves the main road from Uxbridge through Iver Heath. The old established firm of Cravens Railway, Carriage & Wagon Company Ltd. of Sheffield completed one hundred and twenty bus bodies for the Executive which were given body numbers 2681 to 2800 coded RT3/4 with corresponding fleet numbers RT1402 to RT1521. Unfortunately these interesting variants of the RT class were all withdrawn from London passenger service before the end of the year under review. (J.Gascoine collection)

First entering service in July 1954 from Upton Park garage, RTL1546 moved on to Chalk Farm before being garaged at Willesden in the era covered by this book. On 6th June it operates on the special service between Morden Underground Station and Epsom Racecourse. It clearly shows damaged body panels which will be replaced upon it receiving its first overhaul in August 1958 or sooner if the garage body specialists find the time. The Park Royal body, an RT8/2 variant, constitutes the ultimate in design of the RT family. (W.R.Legg)

All Leyland 6RT6 type in the shape of RTW188 is seen at Liverpool Street while engaged on Route 11 awaiting departure to Shepherds Bush, Wells Road. This particular route was associated with this class of eight feet wide vehicles for many years. The conductor is engaged in conversation with an inspector beneath the awning of the tobacconists shop, a facility nearly always found near railway stations but now almost extinct with the current attitudes with regard to smoking. (C.Carter)

A row of eight delicensed Craven bodied RTs are stored inside the vast interior of Stockwell bus garage which had been opened in 1952 as part of the south London tramway replacement scheme. The garage never did operate to its designed capacity of 200 vehicles which allowed other uses to be made of the spare space. In 1956 these seven year old buses, which were superfluous to requirements, were stored there and also at Shepherds Bush garage. From nearest the camera RT1456, 1441, 1440 and 1453 can be positively identified. (John Gascoine collection)

"Passengers" in period costume crowd the top deck of K424, one of a number of London Transport museum pieces which graced the 1956 LGOC Centenary Parade held in Regents Park on Monday 16th July. The celebrations were held between the 16th and 21st July although the actual date of the centenary occurred on 7th January. (D.W.K.Jones)

Standing in front of the older buildings which were the original Amersham garage, GS50 carries duty plates MA17 and has worked down to Amersham off the 394. It displays the typically uninformative layout used for "when working" journeys. This view just shows the standard London Transport RT style brown and green moquette seating provided within the body which carries unmistakable ECW and LT features which complement each other admirably.
(D.A.Ruddom collection)

The Circular Tour of London is being worked by RT2971 on 8th August and it will soon be setting out from Buckingham Palace Road with a full load. Already a queue is forming for the next vehicle to come along. Note the large letter C carried in the canopy blind box. The dolly stop announces the fares and duration of the tour. (W.R.Legg)

RM1 is only weeks away from receiving a revised grille which was fitted at the time the radiator was moved to a more conventional position ahead of the engine. This view is taken on 16th July when the vehicle was taking part in the LGOC centenary celebrations and at the time when earlier alterations had already been put in place. (A.B.Cross)

Connaught Motors acquired three ex-10T10 type vehicles as racing car transporters in the earlier months of the year under review. At the Brands Hatch meeting held on the weekend of 13th/14th October they all appeared together. Although tightly packed in and surrounded by other visitor's transport, this photograph of them was obtained on the 14th. From left to right T711, T682 and T683 now all carry their new owner's name but unfortunately they were all for sale in July of the following year eventually going their separate ways. (A.B.Cross)

On 21st February 1951 new route 203 was introduced to run between Hounslow Central Station and Hanworth, Duke of York, using STL class vehicles operated by Hounslow garage. In a gradual process of expansion by 1956 it was operating between Twickenham and Staines and on 27th June it was further diverted to run into Staines via Stanwell and Town Lane replacing Route 162. A Sunday service was introduced at the western end between Staines and Stanwell. RT1128 with duty plates AV3 is seen in Staines. (W.J.Haynes)

On 2nd August nicely presented RT996 is seen in Eglington Road, Swanscombe, before journeying over to Kings Farm Estate by way of Route 488. This vehicle was allocated to Northleet garage for something approaching seven years which was quite a stable situation for a vehicle of this type in this period of their operating life in London. It is notable too for carrying a very localised advertisement along its offside. (L.W.Rowe)

A recent shower on 6th June has made the road glisten at Reynolds Close, Hackbridge as RT805 operating as A4 on Route 151 awaits its next journey. The destination blind still needs to be reset for its return to Morden or North Cheam. This RT re-entered service from Sutton garage in May after overhaul, having previously been in use at Hounslow from late in 1952. (W.R.Legg)

Standing outside the station at East Croydon, still described as 'Southern Electric', RT492, now carrying a later built body, has stopped for potential custom while in service on Route 194 to Forest Hill as ED26. The date is 13th September and the slogan 'London in 17 minutes' still applies on average today. This bus route's history can be traced back to October 1927 when a Sunday 194 service was introduced between Cheam and West Wickham matched by a weekday 494 between Wallington and West Wickham. (W.R.Legg)

At Ruislip Station RT1150, operating from Uxbridge garage, awaits patronage for the journey to Uxbridge Station by way of Route 220. The section of route northwards to Northwood covered by the first two lines of the blind only operated in peak hours and Saturday/Sunday afternoons. This would be the last full year of this 220 route, it being withdrawn in January 1957. (D.A.Ruddom collection)

RF3 now carries the new uninspiring private hire colours received in June 1955 upon its first overhaul. During 1956 it spent all its time garaged at Northfleet and with no other work for it just now, it is put to good use as NF70 on Green Line route 702 making its way to Sunningdale having arrived at Victoria from Gravesend. Judging by the heavy load carried by the 27'6" long vehicle, the extra four seats provided by a standard Green Line coach would have been an advantage. An unidentifiable RT operates as a relief on another route, again with a good load of passengers. (Roy Marshall)

Route 316 was converted to GS operation on 11th July, being part of the last Country Area summer programme alterations, which in 1956 were spread over several months. GS17, after being garaged at Leatherhead since new in November 1953, now finds itself operating from Two Waters having been returned to service from overhaul in July. It is pictured in the still very basic Hemel Hempstead bus station in September, which was then the terminus before the route was extended to Highfield, Paston Road in October. It could hardly have been envisaged at the time that this bus would re-enact its 316 duties in the hands of preservationists some 36 years later. (P.Gulland)

GS17 was featured in the 1954 book of this series when operating from Leatherhead garage, its first home. With the conversion of some of the quieter Country Area routes which took place in July, this little modified Guy Vixen chassis carrying a 26 seat ECW body, made the move to Two Waters specifically for use on Route 316 which was operated jointly with Rover Bus Services. The bus is now in the capable hands of the GS17 Preservation Group and has on occasion in recent years been seen posed at this very spot in Chesham Broadway. Included in this 1956 view are a Ford Zephyr first registered in May 1956 with a baby Austin in front of the RF operating on Route 394. (F.W.Ivey)

Carrying WR garage plates although officially a Tunbridge Wells garage vehicle, RF61 waits at the western end of Route 704 before embarking on the 199 minutes journey to the Kent spa town. As with several Green Line routes of the time, the schedules were such that vehicles often ended their day at the other end of the route hence the interchangeable allocations. Having received its first overhaul in June 1955, being outshopped with its original body, it still looks in splendid condition some eleven months later when this view was taken. (P.Gulland)

This view, taken inside Aldenham overhaul works in August, clearly shows the very high finish of the vehicles almost ready to resume their daily duties plying the routes of London Transport. At this stage of their visit they have reached the window cleaning area and have little more to be dealt with before emerging in their shining new paintwork. The only vehicle identifiable is RT1038 which resumed operations from Watford High Street garage after this its second overhaul, having been new in December 1948. (P.Gomm collection)

With nearside advertising for free trips to the Olympic Games courtesy of the News Chronicle, RT4722 pulls away from Watford Junction Station bus stop while in use on Route 385A which was introduced on 11th July. An end to end blind is provided for the 21 minute journey of this variant of Route 385 which ran from a previously unserved part of Watford north of Bushey Mill Lane, across the town to venture down Tolpits Lane to the recently completed Holywell Estate. Despite its pleasant name this estate appears to have been built on part of the site of the former Holywell Sewage Farm which was on the opposite side of Tolpits Lane from the Cassiobridge Sewage Farm! (R.Wellings)

A superb conversion from front to centre entrance has been carried out on ex-LT1007 since leaving London Transport ownership in August 1950. The proud owner would appear to have spent many long and loving hours turning this thirty five seat bus into a mobile home complete with hinged windows, an excellent paint finish reminiscent of a turn of the century railway carriage and white wall tyres. The chimney and roof rack rather spoil its beautiful appearance. Its service in London was largely at Muswell Hill interspersed with spells at Holloway, Kingston and Hounslow. (L.Housden collection)

At quarter past five on the War Memorial clock and RT3615 waits beside Rainham Church before departing for Tilbury, Feenan Highway. Grays garage was only the second home for this bus which, between entering service in November 1952 and receiving its first overhaul in March 1956, had resided at Staines. (M.Rooum)

J.H.Dewhurst Ltd., "high class butchers", were once a common sight in many towns and cities until recent times and RTL1007 waits outside this nicely tiled branch at Burnt Oak. Since the shops are closed and the bus is terminating at Brook Road, Borehamwood this picture was probably taken on Easter Monday, 2nd April. This assumption is made since this weekdays only route operated a special service on Easter Monday and on 27th June it was extended in Borehamwood to Rossington Avenue. This version of 52A had been introduced on 30th November 1955 as a localised section of 52 worked by Edgware and Willesden garages and was replaced by 292 under the trolleybus conversion scheme of 3rd January 1962. (F.W.Ivey)

On the 10th June what was once STL2695 passes the Palace Theatre in Victoria Street, Grimsby. Now Grimsby Corporation number 45, the bus works Route 1 to the neighbouring town of Cleethorpes. On 1st January 1957 the new Grimsby-Cleethorpes Joint Transport Committee was formed and the six ex-STLs owned by Grimsby Corporation were to be regularly used in service until the mid 1960s. (J.C.Gillham)

Red liveried RT319 was adopted by the Country Area for the period April through to August and operated from Crawley garage. Here it is seen at Roffey Corner operating the long standing short working on Route 434 from there into Horsham, a journey of nine minutes. The full route to Edenbridge took four minutes short of two hours to complete and was a single deck allocation. (J.Gascoine collection)

The damp cobblestones of the Rennell Street stand in Lewisham provides parking for RT3413 with blinds reset for its return journey to Petts Wood Station over Route 94. The date is 19th August and two months previously the bus had been outshopped from Aldenham after overhaul with this earlier RT3 type body which it was to retain until its next visit in December 1959 when again it would receive a roofbox body but of the RT10 variety. (W.R.Legg)

Although no identification is possible from this photograph it was established that this is in fact the former STL379. The presence of the auto-vac tank indicates that the twenty two year old AEC chassis still carries its petrol engine. Although the body is of similar age it now sits on its fifth underframe. It was photographed in July at Sheerness on the Isle of Sheppey but by the following year the bus had moved to a yard in Mitcham in south west London.

This rear end view of RT4174 in Dartford garage yard shows some minor changes which have taken place within the RT family since the first deliveries were received. The most obvious are the rubber platform mat which has replaced the timber slats and non-slip edging once fitted and the reflectors added to the lower rear. An even smaller change is the used tickets transfer which has been moved from the box to a position above it. The round advert on the corner of the bus is for the London and Manchester Assurance Company – a much less ostentatious approach than the RMC which in later years carried an all over advert in Dartford for the same company. (P.Gulland)

Route 448 with its A suffix variation operated between Onslow Street Bus Station in Guildford and Ewhurst or Pewley Way and received GS class vehicles to replace C class in December 1953. Four GS vehicles were required to maintain the service weekdays and three on Sundays while the 448 route was jointly operated with the Tillingbourne Valley Services. Here GS39 is seen working the very short run of the 448A the vehicle having been one of the initial five delivered to Guildford garage late in 1953, the others being GS30/31/33 and 35. (Surfleet Transport Photographs)

Once a handsome looking "Bluebird" double deck LT which had entered service in July 1932, GX5350 is now reduced to carrying showmen's equipment and towing their living quarters. Once LT1402 plied the streets of London, initially from Hanwell garage, carrying its LGOC built 60 seat body with blue seating. It was withdrawn from service in August 1949 and disposed of to Daniels of Rainham the same month. It is seen here with abundant body sag at Canvey Island on 27th July. (W.R.Legg)

This Leyland Tiger TS3 hides its ancestry admirably, only its radiator suggesting that a closer inspection might be worthwhile. It transpires that the rebodied chassis was once registered GN5140, being one of a fairly large fleet of single deck Leyland TD1s and TS3s taken over by the LPTB on 20th December 1933 when the business of The Premier Line Ltd. of London and Slough was acquired. At the time of acquisition a London Lorries rear entrance coach body seating 26 passengers was carried and the vehicle was given the fleet number TR29. Withdrawn from service in 1938 it was then disposed of to P.M.Morrell, a dealer whose business address was in Leeds, eventually to reappear being operated by C.Taylor of Shillington, a coach operator. After passing through the hands of several other operators it was purchased by Edward Thomas of Ewell in 1949 in whose livery it is now seen on 21st May. Later in 1956 it moved on to a further operator. It is not known when it was rebodied or re-registered but this is a fine record of a vehicle which started life in 1931 and now stands at a well patronised refreshment stop served by London Transport buses and coaches. The rear view shows the typical signwriting used on the rear of coaches at the time. (A.B.Cross)

Deserted RTL1104 with garage duty plates F7 waits at Epsom on Route 93 before returning to Putney Bridge Station. This bus dates from January 1951 when it first entered service for a very short spell from Nunhead garage, whose association with Leyland buses was only a temporary expediency lasting about three months. Since its overhaul in March 1955 it has been allocated to Putney Bridge garage. (John A.S.Hambley)

A bright sunny winter day with the market town buildings of St. Marys Square, Hitchin providing the pleasant background for RT1095. The via blind demonstrates the maximum use of the space available by the compilers and all credit must be given to the conductor for lining it up so admirably. The 303A route deviated from the parent route to serve Welham Green and the village centre of Brookmans Park between Hatfield and Potters Bar. (R.H.G.Simpson)

Were you there at the Centenary Exhibition held on Horse Guards Parade on Saturday 21st July? The bus is K424 and with so many interested onlookers milling around, this view taken above their heads may bring back a happy memory or two to somebody. The gent in front of the radiator was obviously puzzled about something! (G.R.Mortimer)

This fine line up of part of the LTE preserved vehicle collection was photographed inside Reigate garage on 23rd September. This was a much sought after view by enthusiasts at the time since it was not until 1963 that the British Transport Museum in the former Clapham bus garage enabled them to be seen publicly on a regular basis. From right to left we can see B340, S742, NS1995, ST821, LT165, STL469 trolleybus No.1, ex-West Ham Corporation tram No.290. and ex-LCC E/1 tram No.1025 with single deckers beyond which can be seen in a later picture in this book. Most of the vehicles had been used during the summer celebrations of the LGOC centenary which may explain the open bonnets as their curators ensure no damage has been caused by their exertions. (J.C.Gillham)

RTL1446 stands in brilliant sunshine on the cobbles of Athol Street and brightens up this neglected corner of the East End of London much devastated in the war years. Presumably its last duty on Route 108A was in the dark since the lower saloon bulkhead blinds are firmly drawn, unless the driver preferred this for negotiating the dim interior of the Blackwall Tunnel. (P.Gulland)

NLP635 was again taken on loan by London Transport from January 1956 through to May 1957 having previously been seen in the capital between July 1953 and April 1954. This return visit was connected with trials of the new "Monocontrol" transmission which had been developed by AEC to replace the pre-selective gearbox. The vehicle was garaged at Reigate for the sixteen months of its second loan period and was used exclusively on routes 447 and 711. A set of flashing indicators, one of which is visible behind the cab window, have been added since its earlier visit and the bus is pictured at Caterham while in use as duty RG27 on Route 447. (John Gascoine)

Five ton tower wagon 733J was once STL9, numerically the lowest of the class to have been converted into a service vehicle. As a bus it first entered service for the LGOC in March 1933 from Clay Hall garage. By the time of its withdrawal from passenger service it was operating from Potters Bar garage and re-emerged from Chiswick Works in its new guise in October 1949. The superstructure was actually older than STL9, dating from April 1930 when it was carried on an ADC chassis. It was withdrawn in February 1959, being disposed of to A.E.Shurey of Cranford, Middlesex. (John Lines collection)

Three of the buses belonging to the London Transport Collection make their way home after the LGOC Centenary Exhibition on Horse Guards Parade on 21st July. Emerging from Great George Street into Parliament Square they face the Westminster Clock Tower, which at the time was clad in scaffolding. STL469 displays a trade plate to cover its use on the highway while NS1995 follows the lead vehicle which is K424. STL469 also carries a full set of blinds but nowadays the bus has been returned to the restricted display it carried at the time of its withdrawal from passenger service in January 1954. Two Ford cars and a number of cyclists complete an unusual picture. (G.R.Mortimer)

RT446 is now fitted with Park Royal body number 1546 having originally entered service in November 1947 carrying an almost identical Weymann body number 1695. Up until its second overhaul, received in July 1955, the bus had been a permanent resident of Potters Bar garage but re-entered service from Turnham Green. It is seen in use on Route 65 before departing from Argyle Road, Ealing for Hook, White Hart as duty V6.

RT1499 lives on today thanks to the dedication of a trio of hard working preservationists, being one of only two Craven bodied RTs known to survive. The bus is pictured still wearing its Central Area livery prior to being repainted into more suitable colours for its spell of operation in the Country Area. Watford High Street garage was to be its last home before being withdrawn from passenger use at the end of the year. It is seen at Watford Market Place on the corner of Market Street and High Street while working Route 385 between Croxley Green and Mill Way Estate. Neither of the two buildings in the background have survived, more modern structures now standing on this corner.

On 9th August two RTs stand in the lay-by at the New Addington, Homestead Way terminus. They are working the normal 130 service from here to Streatham Common but the bus stop also bears the blue plate for the express journeys on the route which ran between here and East Croydon Station during Monday to Friday peaks and Saturdays. The lead vehicle is RT810 and the route was worked exclusively by Croydon garage. (W.R.Legg)

A number of 2RT2s disposed of by LTE in the previous year were now appearing in service with new owners up and down the country. Ex-RT31 was acquired by Red Rover of Aylesbury in February and given fleet number 8. The roof mounted route number box was felt by many operators to be an unnecessary fitment and removed, often being replaced by a patch, thus spoiling the clean smooth lines of the roof dome. RT31 lasted three and a half years with its new owners but is pictured here on 8th July in this seemingly posed view. (V.C.Jones)

On 6th March, when Route 189 operated Mondays to Fridays between Cannon Street and South Wimbledon with a peak hours extension to North Cheam, RTL854 performs duty roster CA2. Introduced with the second stage of the tram replacement programme on 7th January 1951, partly to replace Tram 6 and also bus 5A, the route was to lose its off peak duties between Clapham Common and Cannon Street on 17th October in the winter programme of service changes. The via point blind is of rather unusual lettering and the Bus Stand has been identified in a very unofficial way on the wooden door of the cycle dealers, whether by the owners or the Executive is uncertain. (W.R.Legg)

RT340 is seen on 26th May operating the fairly short lived Route 239 which ran between Gidea Park, Plough and Romford Station via Eastern Avenue and North Street. The route had been introduced to provide a service on that section of Eastern Avenue between Gidea Park and Pettits Lane but even today this is a rather unlikely area of traffic generation. From its introduction on 30th November 1955 it was a weekday operation but from October 1956 onwards it only worked during Monday to Friday peak hours, disappearing altogether in the August 1958 cut backs. The lone vehicle on the route used the duty number NS190 and this RT3 had been allocated to the Romford garage since its overhaul in October 1955. (B.A.Jenkins)

In the heyday of Route 212 it always seemed that as soon as a bus had taken off down Muswell Hill a queue started forming, anxiously willing the next one to move off the stand in the middle of the roundabout. RF320 collects its quota of passengers as it begins on its sixteen minute journey to Finsbury Park from Muswell Hill Broadway. This bus entered service from Muswell Hill garage in October 1952 and has long since lost its shiny exterior paintwork and the old style blind adds to its worn appearance. In December 1957 it will receive its first overhaul, being outshopped to something like its former glory. (A.B.Cross)

Newly overhauled RT3692 is seen at the Cattle Market stop in Kingston on 20th August about to head south for Surbiton with a heavy load of passengers. The Cattle Market was later to be the site of the Fairfield Bus Station. This particular RT was to survive in London Transport ownership until 1970 having completed over seventeen years of service. (W.R.Legg)

Southern Electric still reigns supreme at Hither Green Station in the ninth year of British Railways. RT924 stands beside a highly collectable nameboard in this photograph taken on 19th August. This RT was garaged at Peckham for a comparatively short period of six months before it departed for pastures new, operating out of Uxbridge. (W.R.Legg)

Eight feet wide RTW49 gives the impression of being much wider than RT1340 which is actually of course only six inches less in width. The frontage of Victoria Station with its continental name dropping provides the impressive backdrop to the vehicles. The 52 appears to have avoided its normal stand and is probably heading for the garage. In between the buses an inspector sorts out a member of the public while a crew sort out some type of document. It could have been just the day's runners and riders I suppose! (C.Carter)

From left to right RT2878, RT1579 and RT730 are parked within the Catford garage yard on 30th March, all looking well presented. RT2878 has been in service for a little over a month since receiving its second overhaul and shows up against the two other less shiny examples. The body of RT730 has the sloping down front cab panel above the offside dumbiron; the other two having a distinct upturn in this area which allows them to be fitted to either Leyland or AEC chassis. (W.R.Legg)

This rear view of RT116 parked near to Edgware garage on 23rd March clearly shows its use as a staff bus by the special plate in the brackets fitted to the rear window. Attention is drawn to the various advertising material aimed at staff and now carried in a prominent position where once the conductor would have stood. The mandatory two reflectors which have been added to the lower edge of the rear bodywork are emphasised by their light coloured surrounds. (W.R.Legg)

RTL1081 is captured in busy Euston Road designated as a "ring road" as it makes its way to Roehampton on Route 30 as duty number AF1. This is well before the construction of the Euston Road underpass and the station direction sign on the central lamp post is an interesting item of street furniture. The slip board "To and From the Museums" is no doubt referring to the South Kensington complex but it is possible that the British Museum and others might take exception to such a generality. (P.Gomm collection)

1016J, a towing lorry using trade plates 047GF, coyly hides its ancestry, only the low slung fuel tank and brass dumb iron plates providing a clue that this was once a bus. The chassis used is that of ex-Country Area STL2677 which first entered service in May 1942 from Amersham garage, initially in red livery. The original LPTB built STL17/1 body, number 447, was disposed of to Cohen the London dealer in August 1951 but 1016J did not emerge until May 1955 carrying service fleet body number 9741. The vehicle is seen on 15th April standing outside Catford garage. (W.R.Legg)

Dorking and St.Albans garages each supplied seven RF coaches for the 712/713 Green Line routes which ran between Dorking and Luton or Dunstable. RF196 lays over on the forecourt of Dorking garage before embarking on its 3 hours 11 minutes journey to the Bedfordshire town from which this series of books emanates. The precise date in 1956 on which this photograph was taken is not known but on 11th July these routes were diverted between Borehamwood and Radlett to operate via Theobald Street instead of Allum Lane. (P.Gomm collection)

RTL64 re-emerged from its September overhaul to be allocated to Camberwell having previously worked at West Green and Barking. It now carries the body once mounted on the chassis of RTL54 and is seen on the stand at Thornton Heath on 21st September. Apart from the Saturday afternoon extension to South Croydon this is as far south as the 159 route now went since the Sunday service from Streatham to Old Coulsdon had been replaced by 190 after operation on 29th April. (W.R.Legg)

Route 230 encountered a low bridge at Headstone Drive necessitating low height vehicles and Weymann bodied RLH53 shows well the lines of one of the second batch to be delivered which had polished aluminium radiator shells. Outside advertising was only carried between decks along the sides of the vehicle. In later years advertising appeared on the rear of these buses between decks as no rear destination equipment was fitted emphasising their provincial appearance. (A.B.Cross)

About to depart for Bishops Stortford from Epping Station, to which it had to make a 'double run' from the garage, well laden RT976 is employed on Route 396 which originated as a replacement for the Green Line services withdrawn on the outbreak of the Second World War. Basically the bus looks much as it would have when it first entered service in October 1948 from Hertford garage, although the colour scheme has been revised. It still retains its Country Area livery, being one of the second batch of green RTs received from Weymanns. (M.Rooum)

What was once C59 is now used as a non-psv with Southern Plasterers Ltd. of Hayling Island. A nice repaint job has been carried out on this Short Brothers bodied Leyland KPO3 of 1935 vintage, which must give some idea of the value the new owners place on the vehicle. Unfortunately it is not known how long it was owned or indeed what happened to it eventually. (N.Anscombe collection)

Passing through 'olde-world' Bushey en-route for Ruislip Lido, RT208 operates from Harrow Weald garage, having commenced its 67 minutes journey at Watford Junction. This RT has already had two overhauls and still manages to hold on to an RT3 type body as originally fitted when it entered service from Potters Bar garage in November 1947. In February 1958 the bus, along with a number of other surplus members of the class and a lesser number of RTLs, was despatched to Ceylon. (R.Stanmore)

With the familiar background of Reigate garage RF69 almost appears to be taking part in an official photocall. This coach was transferred into Reigate garage upon its return from its first overhaul in July 1955 having previously been at Amersham. The front route blind, set for its long journey to High Wycombe on Route 711, makes the point that Oxford Circus is the main via point in Central London. (P.Gomm collection)

On 29th April Cricklewood garaged RT1373 with Saunders bodywork stands in Rennell Street, Lewisham before returning to Willesden garage on Route 1. When Vanguard first gave their routes numbers in 1906, that running between Cricklewood and Elephant & Castle was given the prestigious number 1. So it was that the premier London route number has always been consigned to a rather circuitous route today reduced to being only an inner south east London operation between Tottenham Court Road Station and Surrey Quays. (W.R.Legg)

RT2132 on Sunday route 77B passes the familiar architecture of Sir George Gilbert Scott's Grand Midland Hotel first opened in 1874 with the incline to the higher road level of the forecourt rising at an oblique angle. Since 1935 this Victorian extravagance has been used as offices but in its heyday a night in one of its 600 beds must have proved a romantic end to any train journey. The bus, seen on 16th September, was returned to service from its July overhaul carrying a roofbox body and was allocated to Merton garage having previously spent its earlier years at Uxbridge. (W.R.Legg)

Victoria Station forecourt on 14th October finds RT3697 and RT4083 waiting their respective departure times for Cricklewood, the Crown and Mill Hill, Green Man. The old LGOC bus stops have been adapted for modern use and the original departure light signals have been removed as a comparison with the picture on page 135 of the 1948 book of this series will show. The 16 route between Victoria and Cricklewood was one of the original consolidated and numbered routes of November 1908. (W.R.Legg)

The date is 9th June and Holloway's RT502, still looking in pristine condition from its overhaul received in November 1955, waits at the Putney terminus before returning northwards on Route 14 to Hornsey Rise. There is little else to be said about this typical view of the very standardised bus scene which prevailed in London in 1956. (W.R.Legg)

Heading into London from Stratford along the A11, well laden RT1807 still has some way to go before reaching its destination of Victoria. Trolleybus wiring for Routes 661, 663 and 695 is strung across the road but there is not a silent giant in view. In 1958, with the upheaval of bus services following the lengthy strike and after receiving an overhaul in May of that year, this bus would be put into store at Garston for a period approaching twelve months. (J.G.S.Smith collection)

Now wearing Country Area green on 20th May after its previous month's overhaul, RT1491 works a Green Line relief duty at Eccleston Bridge. Surprisingly in October the still newly overhauled bus was withdrawn from service to become a further addition to the Craven bodied batch of 120 which were to become the first post-war RTs sold. The lucky recipient of this seven year old was eventually to be Wass Brothers of Mansfield. (W.R.Legg)

In use on the circular Route 426 and operating out of Crawley garage, T784 carries a good load of passengers. It was back in 1953 that the delivery of further new Country Area RFs to Garston enabled the allocation of a number of 15T13s to the West Sussex base, bringing the type to the southern area of operations for the first time. (Surfleet Transport Photographs)

The supplementary summer service on Route 74 between Camden Town and Baker Street has over the years been most commonly provided by Chalk Farm garage although several others have lent a hand. In 1956 however the two vehicles needed for the Monday to Friday service were beyond the means of the local garages and Brixton came to the rescue. RT3958 operates as BN2 and a number of excited children accompanied by their parents quickly make for the lead vehicle, which, judging by the posture of the driver, is soon to depart from the stand in Buck Street, Camden Town. (J.Gascoine collection)

Now nearing the end of its distinguished career as a mobile road safety exhibition unit with the Essex Police force, ex-LT1217 stands in the late afternoon sunshine at a convenient parking area in the Essex town of Billericay on 26th August. One small boy is outnumbered by at least three police constables as they converse with each other on the platform of the LGOC designed and built body of 1932 vintage. It was to be withdrawn from this use in 1957 and sold at auction eventually to be used as an open platform lorry. What a pity this was a little too early for the preservation movement. (F.Church)

Newly overhauled RTL26 resumed operations from West Green garage after it emerged from Aldenham in May carrying body number 4425 which had been first fitted to RTL35. The finish of the paintwork indicates the very high standard then given the passenger fleet from London Transport's own workshops, very much in line with the quality produced by the body manufacturers, which in this case were Park Royal Vehicles. Unfortunately the bill posters have not achieved the same standard and presumably there was another bus operating in London proclaiming "KIA KIA" on its front advert spaces! There are plenty of pedestrians but very few buses in this summer Sunday scene at Victoria. (W.R.Legg)

RF683 is parked in the new Hemel Hempstead bus station which had been opened on 4th January. It is on the joint LT/Rover service 316 prior to the London Transport duties being converted to one-man GS operation, which conversion took place on 11th July. However, a "Pay As You Enter" sticker is displayed at the top of the nearside windscreen, so either the bus was a premature conversion or an odd working! (R.Wellings)

Limited stop service 345 operated one return journey on Wednesdays and Sundays between Watford High Street L.T.Garage and Napsbury Hospital and was introduced in 1953 for the benefit of hospital visitors. The buses spent their two hour layover discreetly parked in Caledon Road on the Sheephouse Farm Estate and on this occasion it looks as though duplication was needed. The lead vehicle is RT619 while the one parked close behind escapes identification. A non-roof box body mounted on an HLX registered bus clearly ensured that at least the bus was not sold off in the next round of RT disposals. (J.G.S.Smith collection)

En-route for Chertsey on Green Line Route 716 from Hitchin, RF122 garaged at Addlestone, operates duty roster number 67. The side route board appears to be devoid of any route details. This may just be due to the fact that the gold lettering on green was always difficult to capture on black and white film but it does seem to be exceptionally so in this case. This RF had originally entered service in February 1952 from East Grinstead garage but since receiving its first overhaul in December 1955 has resided at its new address and was to do so until its next visit to works which took place in September 1959. (R.H.G.Simpson)

The old Hertford Bus Station, also known as "Hertford Car Park", long before it was submerged beneath shops and multi-storey car parks. It must be hospital visiting time since GS19 nearest the camera appears to have taken on board a full complement of passengers for its journey on Route 333B to Ware Park Hospital, formerly known as Ware Park Sanatorium, with a number of intending passengers resigned to waiting another 12 or 13 minutes for the next bus. In the background GS74 is waiting to depart on Route 388 to Welwyn, Prospect Place. It is pure conjecture but this could be a Sunday afternoon and the 333B is the 2.21 departure, the 388 the 2.12 departure and the 327, just visible behind, is the 2.19 departure for Nazeingwood Common. (B.Moore)

The word 'ONLY' to denote short workings on destination blinds mushroomed through the system in the very early 1950s but was soon out of favour, being used very often in the wrong context. However in 1956 the odd example could still be spotted as on RT805 at Morden Underground station on 6th June. This bus had been relicensed for service the previous month to operate from Sutton garage after its second overhaul. (W.R.Legg)

A lively view of various other vehicles keeping RTL922 company is afforded by this panoramic picture. From left to right a Ford Thames light van with a rare van version of the Morris Oxford Series MO immediately behind the RTL which waits on the South Kensington stand of Route 45 before departing for Farringdon Street. Parked at the kerbside beside the bus is a Luton van bodied Morris or Austin, badged accordingly to keep the dealers happy in similar fashion to present day practices of some Japanese manufacturers who have interests in a British factory. (A.D.Packer)

Climbing to the bridge over the railway at Barnes Station RT2318 from Hounslow garage on Route 33 makes its way to its home town in the early part of the year just as new leaf buds break out for spring along Rocks Lane at Barnes Common. The 33 route number disappeared from this road for eight years after November 1958, even being re-used in east London during this period, but it returned and still runs along Rocks Lane today as it first did in March 1912. (R.Stanmore)

RF84, a resident of Dartford garage, operates on the southern orbital route 725 between its home town and Windsor. The hourly route had been introduced in Coronation year on 1st July providing the first cross-country Green Line service, operating between Windsor and Gravesend. On 28th April 1954, as a result of the route's undoubted success, the frequency was increased to half hourly between Dartford and Windsor and an allocation of Green Line work was introduced to Dartford. Since the DT coaches were not normally scheduled through to Gravesend, the side boards provided omitted that part of the route. (P.Gomm collection)

RF318 stands on the ramp which led from Hampden Road into Muswell Hill garage having worked in from Route 212 with duty plates MH9. The blind display for these journeys was always rather odd since, although the full route from Finsbury Park to Muswell Hill was worked, only Colney Hatch Lane was given as a via point. Note the use of the route number holder above the entrance, a fitting unique to the Central Area variant of this class as built. (B.A.Jenkins)

Green RLH4 meets red RLH61 at Rayners Lane Station while both were in use on Route 230. On the RLH class vehicles the lack of any rear blind equipment provided the advertising department with an additional space to let. Almost as an afterthought, an older style oblong route number stencil was provided at the top of the rear platform window. (F.W.Ivey)

Ex-RT140 went into service with C.J.Smith (Bluebell Services) of March in August, having been expertly repainted and adapted for its new role operating in and around this market town in the Fens with the old course of the River Nene flowing through. The bus moved on to a further operator before finally being withdrawn for scrap in 1961. (L.Housden collection)

An Austin saloon with registration letters CJH first issued in November 1936 is about to overtake RT114 whose own index letters first appeared in 1939. It must be said however that although the bus was completed at Chiswick Works on 9th April 1940, it did not enter service until 1st September 1941 from Chelverton Road garage. One of those allocated to the Country Area for Route 327, it is seen here at the Fairfax Road stop near Hertford garage while on Route 350 to Bishops Stortford. It was eventually disposed of to F.Ridler, a dealer of London, in May 1963.

On 19th September Bromley's RT2852 unloads its party of day trippers on Brighton Marine Drive while the driver stretches his legs and poses for the cameraman. Farther along the road Maidstone & District's 1954 built Leyland PSU1/15 carrying Harrington bodywork and fleet number CO229 also arrives at the sunny seaside. Samuel Goldwyn's film version of the musical 'Guys and Dolls' in Cinemascope starts showing at the Empire Cinema, Leicester Square on this very day although those inside the bus presumably won't be there. This RT eventually found further service in Ceylon when its days with London Transport came to an end. (J.G.E.Nye)

An unusual compulsory bus and request coach flag, with a plate proclaiming that the stop is an alighting point only for coaches, is surrounded with activity as Green Line RF227 passes through Welwyn Garden City on its way to the Lemsford Lane terminal of Route 372. The picture affords a fairly clear view of the arrangement and fitment of the brackets normally covered by the Green Line route board they are designed to hold. (A.B.Cross)

The Victoria Green Line stand by vehicle for a while in 1955/56 was former private hire coach RF24. It had received this rather cheerless livery in place of the previously carried green and grey at the time of its first overhaul in May 1955. A Green Line service coach must have come to grief on Route 705 and the substitute has reached Sevenoaks, the blind being reset for the return to Windsor. The driver appears to be viewing his controls with some misgiving before lighting up his cigarette. (P.Gomm collection)

Saunders bodied RT1358 passes through Victoria on Route 36 which then operated between Hither Green and West Kilburn as it had done since 1914. Peckham garage, where this RT resides, operated the route which they had done since their opening day in 1951. Nowadays London Central have responsibility for the service which still journeys from West Kilburn, now described as Queens Park Station, as far as Lewisham but the buses required for the service come from New Cross garage. (R.Stanmore)

An interesting picture which shows green liveried RT93 entering Hertford while GS21 leaves in the opposite direction on Route 389 for Gilston. This was a short journey only made once a week on Saturdays, departing from Hertford at 1.03p.m. The bus returned to Hertford from Gilston as a duplicate to the through 1.33p.m.journey from Sawbridgeworth which left Gilston at 1.45p.m. On 17th October Route 388 was extended to Sawbridgeworth in place of Route 389 and this rare working continued as a 388 except that the return journey from Gilston was shown in the timetable three minutes ahead of a through journey from Sawbridgeworth to Welwyn. A Vauxhall car manages to squeeze past the bus while behind the buildings of Christ's Hospital School for Girls add character to the scene. This was the 'Bluecoat' school and the costumed figures over the distant gate posts and in the niches of the wall date from 1697. (F.W.Ivey)

By 1956 Route 366 was operated by one RT supplemented by a second on Saturdays and here, towards the end of RT1476's two short stays at High Wycombe garage, the vehicle displays blinds and running plates HE9 for the route which operated between High Wycombe garage and Widmer End. In August the bus moved into Clapham garage prior to its disposal the same month via a dealer to Dundee Corporation Transport where it was to spend many years of service carrying that operator's fleet number 223. (J.Gascoine collection)

Three ex-London Transport G class buses painted in the main colour of red for Perth City services are parked in the Perth garage yard of W.Alexander & Sons Ltd. awaiting further use. It is an interesting photograph in that three different body manufacturer's products are on view although all have had their original front blind apertures remodelled. From left to right are ex-G198 with Park Royal body, Weymann bodied ex-G414 and NCME bodied ex-G298. Acquired in the early 1950s by the Scottish Omnibus Group, they were to give further service for some nine or ten years still carrying their original bodies until the end. (I.Maclean)

Route 81B was introduced on 22nd May 1954 as a direct link between the embryonic London Airport and Hounslow, being the first route to use the newly constructed tunnel beneath one of the runways to the 'Central Enclosure'. In its first year it was merely a summer weekend operation but on re-introduction on 13th April the following year it became a permanent daily route. RT2988 has no chance of clearing this intending passenger load as it already shows signs of being full up. This Park Royal bodied specimen dates from March 1953 when it first entered service from Hounslow garage where it remained until later in the year. (C.Carter)

An interesting view taken in May of various AEC vehicles in Grimsby. The corporation had standardized on this make of chassis in pre-war days although the war years saw the delivery of a number of Guy Arab double deckers. From left to right fleet number 47 is of course ex-STL2692 which, together with five others of the type, was acquired in August 1955. Fleet number 53 is a 1935 built AEC Regent fitted with a 1937 Roe central entrance body which it had received in 1951 in a body swop exercise. Single decker 69 is a Roe bodied AEC Regal which entered service in 1940 and was rebuilt in 1955 from rear to front entrance for its new role as a one man operated bus. The ex-STL is the only example of an 18STL20 that has found its way into the preservation movement and can be seen regularly attending rallies. (Kevin Lane)

RTL36 found itself one of the earlier members of the class to be withdrawn from service and it was disposed of to Birds at Stratford upon Avon in June 1958. The cause of this may have been the roof box body it received in 1956, an almost unique situation at that time only matched by RTL9 and the prototype RTL501. Its Park Royal body, number 2102, had initially been carried on the AEC chassis of RT822 having entered service in September 1948. RTL36's chassis dates from January 1949. Pulham & Sons of Bourton-on-the-Water, Gloucestershire must have reckoned they had acquired a bargain when they purchased the combination in June 1958. The bus presently finds itself parked at West Hampstead Station while it waits to journey south to Addiscombe on Route 59A. (M.Rooum)

From August 1955 through to October 1960 Triang Toys of South Wimbledon were the proud owners of former T656 an LPTB bodied AEC Regal of 1938 vintage. A splendid repaint with new owners identification added even to the triangle at the top of the radiator has turned out as smartly as one of their products. Used as a mobile showroom, not an uncommon practice for quite a number of sold London transport vehicles, this example later passed to W.E.M. Motors a dealer of SW London. (R.F.Mack)

In February 1953 Park Royal bodied RTL1431 carrying body number 6682 entered service from Hornchurch garage. The vehicle was classified 7RT8/2 as were all deliveries of this class from RTL1314 to the ultimate vehicle, RTL1631. In May of the year under review it received its first and only overhaul being returned to service carrying a further Park Royal body, number 4463 which had graced the chassis of RTL73 when new in January 1949. In April 1959 the vehicle was disposed of to Birds at Stratford-upon-Avon being immediately purchased by J.Laurie of Burnbank, Hamilton who gave it fleet number 46. Here it is seen on 6th June at Morden working from Dalston on the special service to the Epsom Race Course. How different from the sort of vehicles, usually awaiting withdrawal, which were pressed into service on this route a few years earlier. (W.R.Legg)

Another view of the new express Route 803, this time taken outside the peak hour at Watford Junction. RT4554 is caught on its express off peak run to Rickmansworth from St.Albans. The slip board beneath the canopy is clearly visible warning that there is a minimum fare of 6d (2½ p) in operation on this route. The bus, which was delivered to the Executive in August 1954, was first put into store at Shepherds Bush garage, eventually entering service from Grays in May 1955. It was transferred to Garston the following month. (R.Stanmore)

RM1 made its long awaited entry into passenger service on 8th February, being garaged at Cricklewood and used exclusively on Route 2 operating between Golders Green and Crystal Palace. Some differences in its external appearance can be seen when compared to views shown in earlier books of this series. The intake grille for a fresh air and ventilating system has been added above the driver's cab which in turn has eliminated the need for the front upper deck quarter drop opening windows. The original blind box apertures have been replaced with ones which reflect the more conventional style associated with London buses, although radically different from the standard RT. The bus is seen at Vauxhall while employed as W16 and making its way to the Crystal Palace terminus. Initially it carried standard adverts rather than those which later proclaimed it as "London's bus of the future". Notice too the flashing trafficator ears which were new in 1956 and towards the end of the year started to appear on RTs and RFs. (D.W.K.Jones)

STL1913 trundling along a road in the Canary Islands has been rebuilt to allow passenger loading from its offside to suit the local rule of the road. A number of ex-London Transport vehicles were exported to this exotic destination, a group of mountainous islands in the Atlantic off the north west coast of Africa which form the Spanish provinces of Las Palmas and Santa Cruz de Tenerife. The various plates carried on the rear of the bus show that it is licensed in Gran Canaria, the square shaped SP plate proclaims the vehicle to be a public service bus (Servicio Publico) and 70 carried within a white circular background indicates the maximum speed in kilometres per hour. Additional width marker lights have been added at roof height to an otherwise indisputedly LPTB designed and built product. (Kevin Lane)

T779 almost looks as if it is enjoying the gentle touch of the conductresses hand as it stands in the sunshine in the still primitive bus station at Hemel Hempstead. The bus dates from 1948 and except for a one month spell operating from the Leavesden Road, Watford garage in 1952 spent its entire Country Area years at Hemel Hempstead. In 1957 the bus found its way to the Central Area and, still in green livery, was housed at Norbiton garage until withdrawn from service in the early part of 1958. The lady wears calf length skirt and looks slightly encumbered with her Gibson ticket machine and money bag to which her budget key is attached. (P.Gulland)

HGC250 was one of seven ex-London Transport Bristol K6As acquired by the Lincolnshire Road Car Co.Ltd. in 1953 and given fleet numbers 979-983/993-994. There is some confusion as to whether two others were purchased (HGC258/9) but in the event these became Hartlepool Corporation numbers H1 and H3 respectively and with the passage of time the true story may have been lost forever. AEC engined ex-B25 stands at Bracebridge Heath in May with stablemates, which are all of the Bristol marque but powered with the more orthodox Gardner or Bristol engine. Except for the rubber mounted upper deck front windows which are now fitted, the vehicle appears to be still in the condition in which it would have been in London. Now it carries fleet number 2111 having been renumbered from 981, while the vehicle to its right, a KSW6G, has been renumbered from 971 to 2139. (Kevin Lane)

The summery garb of the children seems out of place with the rather bleak looking aspect of Blackheath. Always popular with those seeking leisure pursuits this photograph, however, gives the impression of a moorland more suitable to hikers. Craven bodied RT1518 pulls away from the lonely compulsory bus stop with its destination showing as Woolwich Free Ferry although it would appear to be travelling in the reverse direction. (P.Gulland)

Standing in the dappled sunlight at Finsbury Square, RT1921, garaged at New Cross, waits before departing on a short working to Lewisham on Route 21. The registration, LUC1, would fetch a good price nowadays but in 1950 when the bus was first delivered it was not regarded as anything special. The running number NX6 might indicate that this was a Saturday in the early part of the year when the former tram depot had a Saturday only allocation of eight vehicles on the route. However on 26th June NX gained a full daily allocation thereby displacing Old Kent Road whose association with the route went back at least to the days of the First World War. (Roy Marshall)

Private hire RFW13 stands in Guildhouse Street beside the late 1930s structure of Victoria garage on 14th October. This small class of fifteen vehicles registered LUC376 to LUC390 was a combination of AEC Regal Mark IV chassis fitted with Eastern Coach Works front entrance bodies seating 39 passengers. Together with RF1 – 25 they constituted the private hire fleet which had replaced LTC1 – 24 and TF9 although in March of the year under review the last ten RFs were transferred to the Green Line fleet. (W.R.Legg)

RF76 entered service in December 1951 at Hertford. After its first overhaul in September 1955 it was returned to service at Epping garage still carrying its original body, number 7469. In the early part of the year it is seen at the Aldgate terminus of Route 720 ready to depart for Bishops Stortford. The blind did not deign to offer any via points although the coach is traversing the full route which took an hour and thirty four minutes. (R.Marshall collection)

Ex-STD62 was used by T.A.Wright of Southend-on-Sea for two years commencing in November 1955 and used on contract work for the Bata Shoe Company Ltd. before being despatched to F.Cowley the dealer of Salford to eventually re-appear as a lorry. The one hundred STDs delivered in 1937 were always associated with Hendon garage although some operated from Victoria and Cricklewood in the war years and at the end of their life enough were sent to Enfield to operate the 107/107A routes. A lesser known fact is that a number were transferred to Country Area garages for a short period in wartime. (N.Rayfield)

South Merton Station provides the background to RT2536 now garaged at Merton and photographed on 7th June while enroute to Wallington, Clifton Road on Route 157. This bus had first entered service in May 1951 at Norwood garage together with a fairly large number of its contemporaries. Before the year ended however it had been moved into Dalston garage and over the intervening yeras was to be transferred no less than four times before taking up residence at this south west London garage. (W.R.Legg)

This particular RF delivered in June 1952 was employed as a Green Line coach through to December 1966 when it was downgraded to bus work. Having had its first overhaul, RF255 now appears in much need of a wash to rid it of the accumulation of dust and grime it has picked up while in everyday use. Making its way from Ascot to Gravesend on Green Line Route 701, it carries Northfleet garage plates although the two man operated coach was the rightful property of Staines garage, the other operator of the route. (P.Gomm collection)

Standing at Putney Common awaiting a return journey, Putney Bridge's RTL1064 carries a slip board 'To & From Brompton Road', one of the more well known shopping roads which, including as it does the famous Harrods, is a must for visiting tourists. This particular vehicle was a fairly early disposal, leaving London for pastures new in August 1963 to be purchased in due course by Griffin of Leamington Spa in Warwickshire after spending some time on the premises of Birds of Stratford-upon-Avon. (John A.S.Hambley)

RF12, on loan to Dorking garage, is a "strange visitor" to Route 425 operating a short to Gomshall from Dorking North Station. Painted in the drab all over green with red lettering, it is one of the Private Hire coaches of this class now preserved. (P.Gomm collection)

Services in the Aveley, Belhus, Purfleet and Grays areas were much altered or withdrawn in the 16th May Country bus changes. The new version of the 328 route is represented by RT1055 standing by the side of Rainham Church before departing for one of its several new destinations, in this instance Orsett. The broadside advertisement almost reads like a side board for the Grays Green Line routes except for Ilford and Romford. Even the latter place will attract custom on the 370. (M.Rooum)

Country Area bus T796 was transferred to Grays garage in February 1954 and is now seen here at the Minories Bus Station, Aldgate on Green Line relief duties. The blinds have been reset for its return journey to Grays by way of the normally double deck operated Route 723A which served the Aveley LCC Estate and it carries garage running plates GY105. Parked very close behind is another bus type vehicle on Green Line duties in the shape of RF684 operating from Epping garage. (P.J.Marshall)

When compared to the lower saloon picture of RM1 which appears in Volume One of Ken Blacker's Routemaster history, minor changes can be detected since the vehicle first appeared in 1954. Visible is the heating and ventilation outlet now incorporated into the bulkhead just below the ceiling. The quarter drop opening window originally fitted to the front of the saloon has been removed while, with the new system in place, the two strip ventilators once fitted above the bulkhead windows have been replaced by notices exhorting you to avoid the rush hours when on shopping trips. Standard advertising matter fills the spaces between the unshielded saloon light bulbs. (D.W.K.Jones)

Waiting for its next journey as HD18 on Route 114, Saunders bodied RT1301 is seen at Edgware on 23rd March in company with RT2847. The latter bus is working the preceding duty, HD17, and will be next to leave for Rayners Lane L.T.Station. Judging by the number of partially opened windows on the buses this particular day must have been one of those warmer spring days which everyone looks forward to after the long winter period. (W.R.Legg)

Weymann bodied former G386 was exported to Kenya in 1952 and operated by the Kenya Bus Services, Mombasa, as their fleet number D55. The bus is little changed from its time spent on the streets of London except for some bodywork movement and the rearrangement of the lower deck opening windows. It is seen making its way to the Likoni Ferry having just passed a trio of British servicemen strolling along the footpath in brilliant sunshine. The town of Mombasa sprawls over Mombasa Island and the Likoni Ferry is situated at Kilindini Harbour, the southern of the two harbours on the mainland, which is also linked to the island by a man-made causeway. (R.F.Mack)

The highest number in its class, GS84, although over two years old, has only recently started to earn its keep. Appropriately enough it was the last of the class to do so. Delivered to the Executive in January 1954 it immediately went into store at Garston garage before being moved to Reigate in August where it gathered dust until January of the year under review. With the imminent start of the first overhaul cycle of the class, it was brought into use at Leatherhead garage and is seen here at Epsom Station working the short Route 481 to the Wells Estate. (John A.S.Hambley)

There are two strange things about this photograph of RLH29 on Green Line relief duty at Baker Street. In the first place, appearances of the low height RLH class on such duties was not very common and in the second the 716 did not go to Woking, at least not until 1976 which is well after the days of the RLH! In 1955 the service to Woking was changed from 717 to 716A and perhaps the blind compiler omitted the suffix by mistake and no-one noticed. RT3455 behind is fulfilling similar relief duties on the 711 route to Reigate with correct blinds.

On 28th August RTL986 operating from Chelverton Road, Putney garage is very nicely turned out for its use on Route 28. Standing at Wandsworth Plain in brilliant sunshine it epitomises the superb quality in which the fleet generally operated during this period. (W.R.Legg)

972J stands at Golders Green with the Hippodrome in the background, which nowadays is the home of the BBC Concert Orchestra. The taxi drivers are temporarily inconvenienced while the crew of ex-STL1494 go about their business pruning the trees which divide the bus station from the pedestrian footpath. Judging by all the debris on the roadway they are doing a magnificent job. (D.W.K.Jones)

Red liveried RT904 spent some six months in the Country Area operating from Addlestone garage during the year, having arrived immediately after overhaul in January. Standing beside the railway tracks at Woking Station the bus carries a side blind in the front via box fitted no doubt in the rush to put this handy acquisition into service. Tree pruners have had a field day attending to the two trees which appear to be growing out of the bus roof while Southern Region rolling stock will be identified by railway enthusiasts. (R.K.Blencowe)

Craven bodied RT1425 has now finished its short career with the Executive and is seen standing at the premises of Bird's Commercial Motors in May before delivery to the Ayrshire Bus Owners Consortium the following month. Having entered service in April 1949 from Windsor garage its only reallocation occurred in March 1956 when it moved to Watford High Street just two months before disposal. It was to see a longer period in use with its new owners who rebodied the chassis with an earlier Park Royal built body in 1965. This was London Transport number 1424 which had been carried by RT175 when new. One of the very last lovely old Morris Minors, this example registered in August 1934, is parked alongside the RT. (F.W.Ivey)

On a wet 6th June and with a temporary 'dolly' bus stop in evidence at Crystal Palace, RT3567 is parked across the lay-by entrance as it rests before departure on Route 3 to Camden Town. Norwood garage was the home of this particular bus for a little over three and a half years until September 1959 when, following its second overhaul, it was allocated to Leyton garage. (W.R.Legg)

RF44 stands within the confines of Reigate garage's small parking area awaiting a return journey to High Wycombe on Green Line Route 711. Ten years later this coach was one of the batch selected to be refurbished, modernised and reclassified 1/2RF2/5. (R.H.G.Simpson)

Former RT27 has had little attention since its sale by the Executive in December 1955 to W.North of Leeds. Some attempt has been made at removing the advertising between decks and a new fleet name together with ill fitting route blinds have been added to the front indicator boxes. Anderson Bros. (Beeline Services) of Evenwood, Co.Durham had acquired this LPTB bodied bus in Janurary 1956. It was quickly put into service but unfortunately its new lease of life was short lived as it was withdrawn from service permanently in 1958 and sold to Birds of Stratford upon Avon for scrapping in April of the same year. It is pictured with steamed up windows parked within the West Auckland Bus Station. (Real Photographs)

In the 1952 book of this series TF26 can be seen in happier times operating in service from St.Albans garage, but now seen parked at the South Bank site, Waterloo. After disposal by the Executive in 1953 it was next noted in 1955 having been acquired by a private individual and used for the transport of students attending the London School of Economics and being normally parked in Montague Mews, W1 when not in use. It apparently received some adverse criticism from the local residents at the time, which was reported by the press. By 1958 the vehicle was residing at Pepperton Hill in Wiltshire having been purchased by a local contractor via a dealer. In these photographs taken on 14th February it carries a GB plate, which poses the question how far abroad did it travel? The removal of the rear indicator box gives the body a slight similarity to an LTC coach. (A.B.Cross)

Once their careers with the Executive had ended a number of Qs made their way to Libya for further service. Two examples are shown here and as can be seen from their dual Arabic/English plates are registered LT.9909 and LT.A081. 'L.T.' indicates the registration centre, in this case Tripoli, Zavia and Garian, not the fact that the vehicles are ex-LT! Three of these buses, Q137, Q142 and Q184, are known to have been operated by Guiseppe Cavazzini of Tripoli but unfortunately no one has ever positively matched the registration numbers. A very professional rebuild has been carried out and the vehicles are now left hand drive with saloon entrance repositioned presenting a mirror image of when they had traversed the streets of London. Running plate brackets have gone, one example now carries a bumper with over-riders and both have had marker lights added at roof level but these are only cosmetic alterations and do not detract from the attractive original Park Royal body styling.

Red liveried RT767 is seen in Horsham while in service on Route 434 operating the short working between the town and Roffey Corner. Why this Central Area RT was operated by Crawley garage for some considerable number of months when there were quite a number of unlicenced new green RTs still in store remains a mystery. (R.Stanmore)

On 21st May Tring garaged RT647 takes a well earned rest beside Victoria garage having worked into London as a Green Line relief on Route 706 from Buckinghamshire. Early the following year the bus would be transferred to Garston, its third home, having originally entered service in September 1948 from Grays garage. Now however it carries a much later Weymann body which it gained in 1956 from RT3520. (W.R.Legg)

The Queen's Head at Hoddesdon provides an identification point for RT3501 as it pulls away from the bus stop opposite this fine house of refreshment. The print shows to good advantage the very clear Johnston type face used in the manufacture of London Transport route blinds which far surpasses the front advertisers' use of colour and type. (P.F.Sapte)

Green Line RT3255 was one of the vehicles involved in the experimental fitting of flashing trafficators in 1956 and is pictured at the Minories bus and coach station at Aldgate in September. As with the prototype RMs, a light coloured surround was provided for the fitment, unlike later versions which were in a dark colour. The bus waits on Route 722 to return east as far as Romford (Roneo Corner) from where it will work dead back to its garage at Romford, London Road. (P.Gulland)

Standing at the terminal point for Route 14 in Putney on 4th August with destination blind reset for a return journey to Hornsey Rise, RT751 of 1948 vintage now operates out of Holloway garage. The number blind appears to be an old 14A display with the suffix painted out – a case of waste not want not! (W.R.Legg)

Photographed at Greenford on 4th August, Weymann bodied T760, a stable mate of T755 seen earlier in this volume, shows off its immaculate finish having been returned to service on the first of the month following its July overhaul. A nice Ford is the only car parked along the road, which, parking restrictions allowing, would be filled nose to tail today. Route 211 had its origins in a route of this number from West Ealing to Greenford commenced in May 1931. Although both before and after 1956 it ventured up to Ruislip, its limits in the year under review are defined by the end to end route blind displayed. Nowadays the Ealing Buses 'E' routes cover the service. (W.R.Legg)

Cricklewood garaged RF10 was owned by the Executive from May 1951 through to October 1963, a comparatively short span of years when one considers the length of time for which others of the class soldiered on. As with sixteen others of the initial batch, this vehicle was eventually disposed of to Passenger Vehicle Sales of Ilford and thankfully has now been preserved in the livery in which it entered service nearly forty five years ago. (P.Gomm collection)

Standing within the shadows of the leafless trees in this wintry scene, RT185 waits in the forecourt of Harrow on the Hill Station having turned short on Route 140. The LNER lozenge below the Underground sign set in the glass window above the station entrance has proved too difficult to amend and British Railways have still to make their presence felt. An RT3 type body is fitted and on its further overhaul in March 1957 a similar body, number 1557, would be fitted and this made the bus a candidate for early disposal which took place in June 1963 when it left for W.Norths. (Photomatic Ltd.)

Operating on the intended route after transfer and repaint into Country Area green, RT93 loads from a temporary bus stop in Hoddesdon while en-route to Nazeingwood Common as duty 38. Typical buildings of a market town complete the picture and at the left of the view the covered over permanent bus stop can be seen. The intermediate blind box still carries its masking thereby hiding Broxbourne from view. After its comparatively short term use operating from Hertford garage the bus found itself working as a staff vehicle at Watford High Street before being put to use as the Garston trainer for a while. Eventually it was stored at various Central Area garages before disposal to Bird's Commercial Motors. (A.B.Cross)

RT76 was disposed of to W.North of Leeds in December 1955, subsequently being purchased by International Progressive Coaches of Cambridge in April 1956 and it is seen in company with a Premier Travel vehicle outside Cambridge railway station. Attractively repainted and caught in the late afternoon sunshine, the vehicle would have been a pleasing sight for any train weary traveller. (Photomatic Ltd.)

On 26th June, immediately following its overhaul, RT3491 looks in superb condition being maintained and operated by the staff of Victoria garage. It was photographed at Clapham Common while waiting to take up further duties on Route 137 through the West End to Archway Station at Highgate. This route has its origins in the famous independent Route 536 from Archway to Beckenham and West Wickham operated by Birch and City among others. Renumbered 137 in 1934 its south London destination was changed to Clapham Common in 1937, the onward extension to Crystal Palace being introduced in the following year. (W.R.Legg)

Lancaster City Transport fleet number 459 in ruby and broken white livery was once G319 in the London Transport fleet and is seen having left the bus station on route 7. Four of these Guy Arab II with 5LW Gardner engines were purchased by Lancaster in 1953 but they all had only short careers with their new owners being disposed of by May 1957. (A.M.Wright)

What a marvellous view of townspeople going about their everyday business in a typical off the tourist trail location in southern Yugoslavia. Substantial buildings including the inevitable minaret towering above a mosque dwarfs a familiar sight in the shape of a 10T10. As with so many of these ex-patriot buses the precise identity of the vehicle remains a mystery. (D.Trevor Rowe)

A new registration number system was introduced in Malta on 1st August 1979 using a basic combination of an alpha followed by a number and the letter M in a circle. Prior to this date a simple number only system was in use and ex-TF83 was given the number 3301. Like other numbers in use, 3301 appeared on different vehicles over the years though naturally only one vehicle carried it at any given time. TF83, having been disposed of by LTE to W.North in August 1953 was in use from sometime in 1954 until around 1960 when the number was noted being carried by a Bedford SB1 bus. The unusual 36 seat body was built by a local manufacturer called Aquilina who incorporated some of the original LPTB built panels into its new form. The wheel arches and small lower grille, now lacking its centrally placed foglight, still adorn the body while the front wheel trim disc also helps preserve its London pedigree. Inside the original seats have been replaced by wood framed ones which may have come from London STLs and a rearward facing seat was provided next to the driver. It is operating on the service between Valetta and Rabat.

The first members of the post-war RT class began to be disposed of by the Executive during the year under review. Even so it should be remembered that in 1956 there were still only a small number of the so called 'pre-war' type which had been disposed of while at the same time there was a number of brand new RTs and RTLs still stored awaiting entry into service. Ex-RT1492, with previous ownership and fleet number crudely painted over, stands within the small undercover accommodation provided by Bird's the dealer of Stratford-upon-Avon, before the bus eventually found further service with S.Turner of Brown Edge carrying their fleet number 6. (J.Gascoine collection)

"Ole Bill" as B43 is affectionately known, leads the procession through Regents Park on the occasion of the parade to celebrate the centenary of the formation of the LGOC. This B type bus first entered service in 1911 from the original Clay Hall garage (coded Y) and was sent to France in October 1914, returning to London some five years later in a poor state. Rebodied it was put back into service as a "Traffic Emergency Bus". After withdrawal from service it was fitted with another body and presented to the Auxiliary Omnibus Companies Old Comrades Association. Nowadays it is kept in the Imperial War Museum. The metal figure fixed to the radiator cap gives the bus its name, being a World War I cartoon character. This, together with the polished shell case on top of the dashboard and brass number plate, was added after the vehicle visited Buckingham Palace on 14th February 1920. The names of major battles painted above the lower saloon windows were added when the vehicle was made ready for its glorious retirement. (D.W.K.Jones)

On 28th May Saunders bodied RT4232 waits at Chingford Hatch before commencing a journey to Clapham Common, Old Town on Route 35. Operated by Leyton garage, this bus was normally a resident of Loughton garage. The two garages frequently interchanged their vehicles as needs demanded. (W.R.Legg)

T794 arrived at Kingston garage along with T785 and T796 on 8th August from the Country Area for use on Route 216 and must have been a welcome transfer for the drivers who otherwise had to contend with manual transmission TD class buses, these Ts having fluid transmission and air operated gearboxes. They were to be a familiar sight in and around Kingston for the next two and a half years although they remained in their Lincoln green livery. On 26th August the Wood Street lay-by beside Kingston railway station provides the terminus of the route which worked out to Staines via Sunbury as it does to this day. (J.H.Aston)

During 1955 a number of express bus services started to appear primarily to provide commuters with an alternative to the private car in reaching railway stations thereby making the journey to Central London quicker. Route 174 had an express section running between Harold Hill, Gooshays Drive and Romford Station during the weekday rush hours and on Saturdays for the convenience of shoppers. RT2753 with route blinds consisting of white lettering on a blue background is pictured at Romford Station having been transferred during July from its previous usage at Catford. (A.M.Wright)

In the vicinity of Victoria garage RT3681 takes a well earned rest after operating into the capital as HN206 on Green Line route 716 relief duties on 21st October. Originally entering service in March 1953 this Weymann bodied RT8/2 was one of the Country Area batch RT3647 to RT3683 which were basically placed into service as overhaul replacements. Watford High Street garage was the initial recipient but by now the bus has moved to the northern outpost of Hitchin, once only capable of housing single deck vehicles. (W.R.Legg)

Craven bodied RT1506 received a repaint into Country Area livery in April of the year under review and found a new operating base at Watford High Street until it was taken out of service and put in store at Shepherds Bush garage in November. It is seen arriving at Windsor Guildhall on Route 335 having almost finished its 1 hour 46 minutes trip from Watford. Further service with the Ayrshire Bus Owners Group allowed the bus to complete a similar number of years of service north of the border to that spent with the Executive. (A.B.Cross)

Now painted in green livery, Craven bodied RT1490 works from Staines garage on the special service which operates between Staines and Ascot for the benefit of racegoers. Overhauled back in 1953, twenty three red Craven RTs were repainted into Country Area colours in April and May although they were to be withdrawn from passenger service later in the year. (A.B.Cross)

During the period 1953/54 a total of twenty three ex-D class vehicles were acquired by Samuel Ledgard from the LTE via North's the dealer. They were purchased at a time when it was said nothing else was available in quantity on the second hand market and they joined a predominantly all Leyland fleet. One further ex-London D class bus was purchased in March 1956 coming via Bee Line Roadways Ltd. None of these vehicles however survived to overlap the arrival of the first ex-RTs which were acquired in 1963. HGF949, once D272, is from the first batch of fourteen acquired in 1953 and is seen on the Ilkley via Guiseley service running over the Leeds tram tracks and being pursued by a Leeds Corporation Leyland bus. (R.F.Mack)

Another view of an ex-London Transport 5Q5 with registration number LT.A.004 pictured with typical Middle Eastern architecture as a background which is a far cry from its old London haunts. This and the other Qs depicted within the pages of this book were used to transport US service personnel when on leave between Tripoli and the huge military base at Wheelus Field, a most untypical African name if ever there was one. The Q again has been expertly converted for use as a left hand drive vehicle which begs the question, was this done before export? The pockmarks on the stonework of the building are presumably a legacy of fighting in the Second World War.

Dalston's RF310 is neatly blinded for duties on Route 208 to Bromley by Bow, Seven Stars. Very soon after being photographed this bus would be renumbered RF529 and then three years on would be converted to one man operation, which was when it finally moved away from its Dalston home to pastures new. (A.B.Cross)

This further photograph taken inside Reigate garage on 23rd September shows the single deck vehicles of the then preserved LTE fleet. From left to right, CR14, TF77, Q55 and T219 are parked between tram number 1025 and one of Reigate's serving RTs, 1083. CR14 was later sold to P.J.Marshall in June 1967 for private preservation but has not been seen by the author for many years while the other vehicles still form part of the London Transport Museum fleet. Q55, which these days is one of the reserve fleet not on display at Covent Garden carries the cream relief around the front windscreen. This style was perpetuated in a repaint a year or two back, which is odd since these vehicles had all green windscreen surrounds when in service. (J.C.Gillham)

Ex-D220 was a 3/4D4 while in the ownership of London Transport and carried body number 1243, spending its entire operational life working from Sutton. It was withdrawn from service in February 1953 passing to North the Leeds dealer in the following month. Along with thirteen other ex-D class buses it was acquired by Samuel Ledgard in the same year with a further batch of nine following in 1954. Of the original batch two, including this one, were fitted with platform doors in March 1956 and on 27th May this Park Royal bodied Daimler CWA6 shows off its gleaming dark blue and white livery in Leeds city centre. (J.G.E.Nye)

The registration number CLX591 is recognisable to London Transport enthusiasts and historians as that once carried by STL1343 when it operated in the capital from new in May 1936 until withdrawn in July 1950. It was disposed of to Daniels the Rainham dealer in the same month ostensibly for scrap. However, it is seen here conveniently parked and surrounded by other miscellaneous fairground vehicles on Woolwich Common on 2nd May having been professionally rebuilt for its second life. From May 1949 to April 1951 Daniels had the contract to scrap time expired London Transport buses and coaches and restrictions on the use of any vehicles resold were included in the terms as laid down by the British Transport Commission. No vehicles were to be resold for stage carriage use where they might be in competition with BTC controlled concerns but the vehicle's present use does not appear to contravene these regulations. (W.R.Legg)

Route number 209 remained unused between 4th May 1938 and 14th May 1952 on which date a new service between Harrow Weald garage and South Harrow Station via some previously unserved roads was introduced using STL type buses from HD. By 1956 the STLs have been replaced by RTs and here at South Harrow Station the new order is represented by RT1900 operating as HD5. (D.A.Ruddom collection)

In March and still some several months before delivery to the Executive, the vehicle which was eventually numbered RML3 is seen at the Weymann bodybuilders' premises in Addlestone. The "L" indicated the Leyland mechanical units used on this vehicle rather than the later vehicle length significance. At this stage the body was just a shell, no fitting out having taken place and the vehicle is finished in grey primer except for the bonnet which is a glass fibre moulding. Improvements in the bonnet area have been incorporated and, unlike the first two prototypes which were hinged at the rear, this example is of the side lifting variety which, as it turned out, was unique. The much narrower design, which greatly improved nearside kerb visibility for the driver, was perpetuated in the production vehicles. (G.A.Rixon)

Beside the passenger vehicles, some service vehicles took part in the Centenary of the LGOC parade in Regents Park and on that day, the 16th June, ex-STL197, now identified by its service vehicle fleet number 737J makes a nice subject for the camera of D.W.K.Jones. The square paper sticker describes the vehicle to be a 'Master Breakdown Tender' for the benefit of any less well informed people watching the parade. Trade plates 016GH are now carried in place of the more familiar AGX538. The rear wheel trim now fitted would not have been in place in the vehicle's passenger earning days but was probably added by Cricklewood garage to enhance the shortened vehicle in its new role. (D.W.K.Jones)

Uxbridge garage always provided the vehicles required to operate Route 225 ever since its inception on 26th January 1944. From small 20 seat OMO Leyland C class buses the route has grown in stature to using 56 seat double deckers represented here by RT2559 working duty UX103. The driver rests his chin in his hand as he lays over at Northwood looking suitably bored with his almost straight run through Eastcote to Eastcote Lane. (R.H.G.Simpson)

Well photographed C82 appears again in the pages of this series of books but this time as some sort of fairground transport in York on 16th August after having been initially disposed of by LTE in September 1955 to W.North of Leeds. First entering service in April 1936 it was to be eventually withdrawn from passenger work in October 1953 and put into store for a few months before its next task as Plumstead's staff bus which lasted for a little over a year. It then went into store once more before its disposal. It was last reported at a showman's winter quarters at Stainforth, Yorkshire in the middle of 1965 and at that time, like all grand old ladies, was taking life easy. (Lyndon Rowe)

In 1953 Burton Corporation acquired six ex-London Transport G class vehicles of 1945/46 vintage through the Leeds dealer North to replace newer single deckers on routes now suitable for double deck operation. The buses involved consisted of G324/339/346/351/415 and 434. HGC125, once G346, was given fleet number 69 by its new owners. All six were reconditioned by Roe prior to entry into service and two of the batch had their bodies rebuilt by the Corporation in 1958. By early 1967 all had been withdrawn after serving more years in operation with their new masters than they did with London Transport.

Presumably after visiting Chiswick Training School GS24 is seen tootling along Chiswick High Road on a rather rarer duty for this type of vehicle. An L plate has been neatly added to the centre of the radiator while another hangs from the cross bar fitted to the rear emergency door. This class of vehicle were fitted with four speed constant mesh manual transmission systems nicknamed the "Chinese" variety as the H shaped gate allowing movement of the gear stick from one gar to another was reversed from the normal order of operation and drivers had to confidently master this little problem before being allowed to use the vehicle in service. (R.H.G.Simpson)

A chance encounter with ex-RTC1 as it proceeds along Walton Lane, Liverpool during murky October weather now shows the vehicle with panelled over blind boxes. Tram lines still pass through this part of the industrial area of the city while only one other vehicle shares the fairly wide roadway. To the extreme left of the picture someone has picked up the different engine note and turns his head in curiosity to look at the vehicle producing the unfamiliar sound of an AEC engine modified to A185B standards. The bus had been bought as a non-runner by W.North of Leeds who had contrived to get it working again before sale to Vernon's Industries of Liverpool, who used it, as here, as a staff bus. (N.N.Forbes/National Tramway Museum)

HGC261, having just been outshopped from the Harkness body shops, looks flawless as it awaits a test run in its new guise. Originally D134 when operated by London Transport between January 1946 and January 1954, it is now plain 535 with its new operator, Belfast Corporation, to whom it would give many years of service, outstripping its years spent on the roads of London. (S.A.Newman)

A roller blind showing route number in place of the previously fitted RT style plate positioned mid-way in the staircase panel is now incorporated into the offside of RM1. The handle to operate the device was carried behind the fare chart door. London Transport, justly proud of their new baby, incorporate the word "Routemaster" in two positions on the offside with a cast plate below and to the right of the fleet number while a transfer is affixed above the second lower saloon window. The trees, devoid of any greenery, indicate the picture was taken soon after the bus had entered service in February. The smaller blind display compared to the RT family was due to the heating and ventilation grille and the attempt to cram four lines of information was a mistake which would be corrected when the production models arrived. The towers of the old Crystal Palace High Level station, by this time disused, loom in the background of this deserted scene. (John Gascoine collection)

Another red liveried RT to be the subject of short term loan to the Country Area in the year under review was RT895 which spent from July through to November operating from Amersham garage. Seen immediately after transfer from Plumstead garage (AM) to its new home (MA) it operates on Route 305 between Uxbridge and Beaconsfield with a mixture of previously carried advertising and added Country Area material. The latter includes publicity for 5/- Rover Tickets which became available in most of the North Division from 1st July. They had been available in the South Division since 20th May. (R.H.G.Simpson)

Route number 332B was a short lived variant of 332 introduced on 14th May 1954 and used for one journey between the new housing at Aveley and Purfleet Station. It was withdrawn on 16th May of the year under review along with the entire 332 group of routes. At the same time 323 and 328 were so much altered that with the introduction of Route 328A the allocation at Grays increased by three vehicles. RT4123 stands between a builders' lorry and uncompleted housing at the Usk Road terminus. This was a scene repeated throughout the Country Area with so much building in progress at the time. (D.A.Jones)

RLH6 entered service in June 1950 being painted green for Country Area service and allocated to Amersham garage. When the time arrived for Merton garage's allocation of the type to receive their first overhaul, which took place in the latter months of 1956, this bus made the pilgrimage south to help out on the 127 route. It is seen here in Milner Road, opposite the Northern Line's South Wimbledon Station during its only sojourn in the Central Area. (A.B.Cross)

The interior of this ST was shown in the 1946 book of this series and now this exterior view has come to light showing the bus parked beside Old Kent Road garage awaiting further service. The vehicle is ST613, repainted in the blue and cream Interstation livery and reseated in December 1943. It reverted to its normal red livery and seating arrangement in June 1946. The blind clearly shows the stations served by this circular operation. (Omnibus Society)

Between December 1942 and February 1946 the Bristol Omnibus Company Ltd. had a total of twelve of these ST class vehicles on loan, comprising numbers ST262, 292, 348, 377, 495, 499, 524, 538, 587, 616, 617 and 629. From January 1944 they also carried Bristol fleet numbers 3830/1/2/4/3/5, 3701/2/3/6/4/5 respectively and nearest the camera is 3701 alias ST524. The bus in the middle is ST616 but it is not possible to identify the other vehicle which has the front bulkhead window surround painted white. (B.E.Speller collection).

A full blind display is carried by STL1729 although the via point blind relates to part of Route 406 and the 424 route was normally operated by Q class single deckers at this time. Parked behind is another STL which appears to have already been fitted with the restricted style of blinds. Although identical advertising is carried along the sides of the buses the front panels are occupied by two rival weekly pictorial news magazines. These were very popular during the war but eventually both were killed off by the advent of television in the post-war era. (B.E.Speller collection).

Canvey and District Motor Services of Canvey Island in Essex owned GN184, a Leyland Titan TD1 with Dodson 56 seat body from August 1939 to June 1943. This bus first took to the roads of London in 1931 being owned by the Westminster Omnibus Co.Ltd. Their fleet was acquired by the LPTB on 10th July 1934 and this vehicle was given fleet number TD95, a diesel engine being fitted in October 1934. Although it was only eight years old it was withdrawn from service in 1939, put into store and eventually sold to W.North & Sons the dealer of Leeds before finding its way to Essex. In icy conditions the driver hurries to the fully laden bus early in the war years. (S.L.Poole)

Obviously this is a wartime picture but nothing is known as to why three ex-Tilling ST class buses should be gathered together with an STL just visible on the extreme left of the picture. No route blinds, boards or duty plates are carried and the location is unknown. Fortunately two of the STs are identifiable; the one with a few boarded up windows being ST882 and the example carrying Swan Vestas advertising being ST862. Your comments would be welcome!

Cumberland Motor Services of Whitehaven was a staunch purchaser of Leyland products before and after the war years until 1954 when the first Bristols appeared. In 1940 a total of thirty secondhand Titans were added to the fleet, seven being ex-LPTB vehicles acquired via a dealer. EV6510 had previously operated in London as TD123 having been acquired on 6th November 1934 with the business of the Reliance Omnibus Co.Ltd. who operated from premises in Folly Lane, Chingford. Still carrying its original Dodson 52 seat enclosed staircase body it serves passengers outside the Whitehaven bus station. Before its final withdrawal in 1954 it had been re-engined in 1940 with a Gardner 5LW unit and received a new Burlingham 54 seat highbridge body in November 1948.
(S.L.Poole)

In January 1939 former Green Line 27 seat coach T179 was disposed of to the Arlington Motor Company in south west London. Later acquired by the General Post Office it appeared in August 1940 carrying new registration number GGJ297 and fitted with this unusual van body for its use as a mobile coastal radio station. Along the bottom edge is the inscription 'Post Office Engineering Department' while the vehicle weight is painted beyond the rear wheels. The offside brass dumb iron plate is still in situ while use of the bonnet cover also gives a clue to its previous origins. Other than the fact that it was scrapped in December 1968 nothing else is known about this interesting conversion. (N.Anscomb collection)

This view of ST778, primarily photographed at Chiswick Works to show available advertising space provides a very fine broadside view of a standard ST. The wheelbase of this type of vehicle is 15'6''' with overall length of 25'0 and 3/8''. The weight of 6tons 12cwts is a hundredweight heavier than when it first entered service in May 1931. Additional body strapping has been added beneath the pillars of the fourth and fifth window bays, probably at the time when the bus received attention at Berkeley Caravans, Biggleswade in October 1948. (L.T.Museum U45246)

This picture of ST1073, originally delivered to the London General Country Services in 1932, is a vivid reminder of the lack of road traffic in 1948. Around midday on 23rd July it stops to pick up passengers in Watford Town Centre while Mr Jones appears able to stand in the middle of the road to obtain his shot. The bus is working Route 345 through to Northwood. When it reaches this point it will perform a U turn at the junction of Rickmansworth Road and Ducks Hill Road in order to return to Watford. Imagine what a manouevre like that would do to the traffic nowadays! (V.C.Jones)

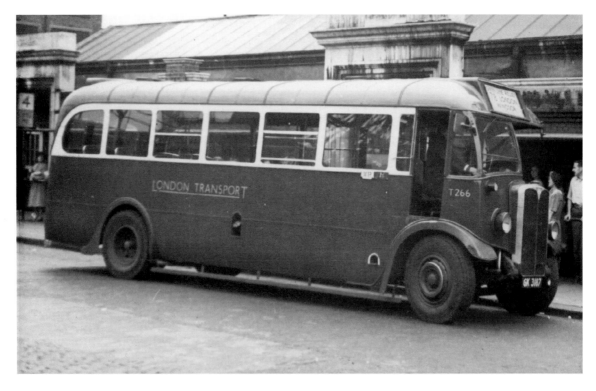

Such was the need for passenger carrying capacity to attractions like Hampton Court and Windsor on Bank Holidays that any available vehicle was pressed into service. Here 11T11 type bus, T266, is seen working as a Green Line relief on Route 718 between Victoria and Windsor, the duty number WR126 giving some indication of the number of reliefs in service on Bank Holiday Monday 2nd August. (V.C.Jones)

RT2 was transferred to Plumstead garage ostensibly for type training duties prior to the allocation of new RTL buses but it is seen here at Powis Street in Woolwich on regular passenger duties. It operates on 27th August 1949 as AM1 on Route 53, which then ran between Greenwich and Plumstead Common via Woolwich Road. At this time LTs were scheduled for the route but this RT, dating from 1940, must have provided a foretaste of things to come on this Saturday. (A.B.Cross)

This Gilford 168OT model with Wycombe bodywork, which first entered service in December 1932 with Edward Hillman's Saloon Coaches Ltd., still gives yeoman service and is seen at Epsom on a day at the races. Originally it had operated as Hillman's No.124 from their Bow Road premises. On 13th August 1934 it was taken over, along with the rest of the fleet, by the LPTB and given fleet number GF112. In 1936 the vehicle was withdrawn from service and stored at the AEC works in Walthamstow until disposed of to Dawson, a dealer in south west London. It was to enjoy further service with several owners before being permanently withdrawn in December 1950. (S.A.Newman)

A picture of T626 appears in the 1953 book of this series but without the filled in offside area below the headlight which had been carried earlier as depicted here in this view taken on 5th October 1949. Operating from Amersham garage passengers are boarding at Chesham for a journey on Route 394 to the quaintly named destination of Chartridge Reading Room, which village was surprisingly served by no less than six different routes at one time. In September 1956 the bus was despatched to W.North of Leeds in whose yard it languished until being scrapped two years later. (A.B.Cross)

A fine view taken from St.Clement Dane's Church shows Mortlake's RT779 on
Route 9 and Dalston's STL2518 both heading for Liverpool Street. The trees are
still decorated with fading white rings left over from the war years.
(B.E.Speller collection).

With the conversion of the chassis of former STL2607 to SRT65, the LPTB body number 175 was remounted on to
STL2069 and the remodelled bus returned to service in April 1949. As STL2607 the body had received full Green Line
livery just prior to the commencement of the 1948 summer season in line with its allocation to Romford, London
Road. Still carrying its former up-market image but with new fleet number transfers it now performs ordinary bus
duties from St.Albans garage where it waits to take up a further journey on the summer route 368 to Whipsnade Zoo.
Odd that in the previous summer in its previous incarnation the body might have reached the same destination on
the 726 Green Line. (A.B.Cross)

RT169 was among the earliest standard post-war RTs to be sold. In January 1958 it went to Bird's Commercial Motors for eventual resale to Cunningham's of Paisley. By that time it had an RT8 type body with which it had operated from Leyton garage. Here it is seen in its original form laying over on Route 130 at New Addington while working from its first garage which was Croydon. (B.E.Speller collection).

The more usual destination shown by buses working Route 354 in St.Albans was the enigmatic "CIRCULAR". This was a strange route in that on each journey the bottom half of the circle between the garage and Fleetville was covered twice. Since anti-clockwise buses reversed their direction on reaching Fleetville for the second time, it was probably correct to show "FLEETVILLE" once you had passed it the first time. STL2146 does just this in St.Peters Street on 26th March. The bus is fitted with the STL16 type body that was originally carried by STL2627, whose chassis was required for the SRT conversion programme. (A.B.Cross)

This photograph of ex-LT1202 dated October 1950 poses a question. The vehicle is one of only four double deck examples completed by the LGOC from an original sanction to build six and carried chassis number CC1002 and LT5 style body number 12599. The original 6 cylinder Meadows petrol engine was replaced by an AEC unit in July 1933 though it retained its distinctive radiator as seen here. Withdrawn from service in May 1939 it was then acquired by the British Broadcasting Corporation in August as a mobile radio transmitting vehicle and in 1947 passed to Billy Smart's Circus. Here in October 1950 it stands in the yard of Birds the dealer at Stratford on Avon where it remained, the derelict chassis still being there in April 1961. The question is: what happened to the vehicle between ownership by Billy Smart's Circus and its acquisition by Birds and who is A.H.Kearsey Ltd.? (A.B.Cross)

A normal resident of Clapham garage, RTL850 is seen while on loan to Watford High Street garage on Saturday 30th June 1951. It is climbing the High Street while working Route 332 between Oxhey Estate and Cassiobury Park Estate. This route was able to travel in a more or less straight line between Bushey Arches and Watford Town Hall. Nowadays a zig zag course is necessary to achieve this, crossing the line of the old High Street at least three times! (A.B.Cross)

With the delightful backdrop of Chesham Broadway a Leyland Cub and a Bedford OB add to the feel of a rural town. The Leyland is London Transport's C38 operating a short journey to Cholesbury on Route 397 which reached Tring Garage on a full service while the Bedford is owned by the Rover Bus Services and is about to depart for Hemel Hempstead on the route worked jointly with London Transport's 316. Less than three years later C38 would be owned by the St.John's Ambulance Brigade, further extending its life which had commenced in June 1935. (A.B.Cross)

RT3255 and RT3228 stand beside the leafless trees in the parking area which lies across the road from Whipsnade Zoo in Bedfordshire. The route blinds with primrose yellow lettering on a green background have been reset for the return journey on this summer route 726 to London, Baker Street worked by Romford, London Road garage. (P.Gomm collection)

In June 1951 the International Union of Public Transport held their conference within the city of Edinburgh. Brand new RT2565 made the long return journey of around 732 miles to take part using trade plate 368H and upon its return to London was licensed to enter service from Upton Park garage. Obviously the opportunity of a photocall at South Queensferry could not be resisted and here is the result – a slight detour on Route 27! The Forth railway bridge, designed by Sir John Fowler and opened in 1890, was of these massive proportions since the Admiralty required headroom and space to accommodate the passage of warships up the firth. (B.E.Speller collection).

C18 traverses the roads of picturesque Beaconsfield on its journey from Penn to Holtspur, North Drive by way of route 373 on 7th October 1951. In 1955, together with others of this class, C18 made the journey to Ceylon to be much altered, eventually seating 41 passengers. (A.B.Cross)

On 8th June 1951 D138 emerges from the stand at the Woodstock public house. This pub still stands to this day at the junction of Stonecot Hill and Sutton Common Road. Once bus stands in pub forecourts were commonplace but nowadays all available space has been taken over by the motor car and very few such facilities remain. (A.B.Cross)

A comparatively large number of G class buses found further use as training vehicles once they had been withdrawn from passenger service. Park Royal bodied G66 was one such vehicle and it performed this useful function from May 1951 until finally finding its way to the disposal pool in Edgware garage yard in September 1952. From there it went north of the border in March 1953 for further passenger service. (Aviation & Transport Photographs)

Route 244 was to become a double deck route on 6th May 1953 to be operated by RT class vehicles and the Leyland single deck TD class buses previously used would be a thing of the past. TD20 stands in Chaseville Park Road, Winchmore Hill, having turned short at Highlands Hospital in the days when single deckers still provided the service. (R.Wellings)

This view of RT154 on Route 74 is included to show the interim black route number plate fitted to the offside of early post-war RT vehicles in 1948. The word "Route" on a black background was added at the time of the vehicle's first overhaul and this RT had received such attention in August 1951, losing the cream surround to its upper deck windows at the same time. Note the deletion of the word "ONLY" on the very cramped destination display for Earls Court, Empress Hall. Note too the bomb damaged remains of Camden Town Underground Station in the background. (A.B.Cross)

These two prints show loading taking place of the MS.Baron Elphinstone at London Docks with a total of sixty seven vehicles destined for Colombo in Ceylon (now Sri Lanka). The vehicles, which include D70 and D109 have the London Transport fleet names painted out in the usual fashion. Together these views give a good atmospheric picture of dock activity at the time. (M.H.Lockyer)

Careful inspection of TF63 and an unidentified 4Q4 both in pink and yellow livery, reveals that they have been converted with offside doorways and are ready for export to Spanish Morocco. The date is 20th July 1953 and the vehicles are parked within Chiswick Works. Does anybody know whether these conversions were carried out on site or sub-contracted elsewhere? (J.C.Gillham)

On Coronation Day it was all hands (or vehicles?) to the pumps and Hendon garage put RT27 their training vehicle on Route 113. It carries the special slipboard to show that Baker Street is its Central London terminal for the day. After returning to normal service at Chelverton Road garage the bus was sold to W.North in December 1955 and later went to Anderson Brothers (Beeline Services) of Evenwood who used it for less than two years. (D.A.Jones)

STL1829 had a history stretching back to March 1937 when it entered service from Forest Gate garage as a 4/9STL14. At the time of its October 1938 overhaul it was given a similar Chiswick built body, number 17086. In October 1947 this body was rebuilt by Mann Egerton of Norwich and it continued to serve Londoners until withdrawn in January 1954, its last operational garage being Alperton. Here it is being handed over on 5th February 1954 to the 6th Royal Tank Regiment, then part of BAOR, garrisoned at Munster in Germany. Eventually it would receive military registration number 402 RB 2 and be named 'Miss O'Garn'. Curiously it has been fitted with an AA badge and it appears that its dumb iron brass plates have already received some military "bull". Pity about the dent – I hope the Sergeant driving had that noted down before he took over! (LT Museum R12)

In October 1953 Chelsham garage placed GS class vehicles in service on Routes 464, 465 and 485 which gave them the honour of being the second garage after Hitchin to operate the type. GS6 is seen on stand immediately outside the George & Dragon in Westerham High Street awaiting departure for Edenbridge as duty CM18 on Route 485. The operating trend as far as this group of routes was concerned had been set and was to last for the next nine years until the arrival of five OMO RFs ousted the GSs on 24th October 1962, a year when it was obvious that the class was on the way out. (R.Wellings)

STL1059 parked in the Crawley garage yard appears confused as to its use, displaying Route 438A on the front blind and 434 on the side. RF530 stands to the right of the double decker which had entered service in July 1935 as the highest numbered in the first batch of front entrance STLs. It was in August 1948 that this STL14 body was mounted in place of the body which had been carried since new. (R.Wellings)

STL1011 in half shade and brilliant sunshine emerges from Crawley garage to take up duties as CY18 on Route 405 which at its fullest extent operated between Horsham and West Croydon Station. It is most likely that this ageing vehicle was only on its way to operate local works journeys in the Crawley area however. In the autumn of 1954 this 4/9STL14, having originally entered service as a front entrance 10STL6, would be withdrawn from passenger service and used as a training vehicle at Clapham garage until its sale to a dealer in the following year. (R.Wellings)

During 1953 all but one of the 66 new GS vehicles so far delivered were now in service. One of the last to enter service in December was GS62 which completed the conversion of Amersham garage routes 348/A, 373, 397 and 398/A. Early in the following year a good number of passengers are about to board the vehicle outside the garage on the 398 service which had started its journey to Beaconsfield at the Quill Hall Estate. (A.B.Cross)

On 17th April 1954 RF197 is seen at the 'Woodstock' bus and coach stop at Sutton Common Road while operating on Green Line Route 713 to Dunstable with much of its journey still to complete. This RF had first entered service in March 1952 being one of an initial batch of eight allocated to St.Albans garage for their involvement in Routes 712 and 713. Here it carries a Dorking garage plate having finished its previous day's duties at the southern end of the route. (A.B.Cross)

Crawley's RF677 waits to set out from the Carfax at Horsham on Route 434 as far as Dormansland. The section further on to Edenbridge was often worked only by buses from Turners Hill or Crawley. The blind belies the length of the route. Even this section took an hour and a half and the many places served, including East Grinstead, do not get a mention. This RF had entered service the previous year and still looks almost in as delivered condition. (Surfleet Transport Photographs)

In the early part of the year a trio of withdrawn T class vehicles are seen in the Dartford garage yard collecting dust. From right to left we have T615, T627 and T635. The first two were disposed of soon after this photograph was taken while T635 was stored at two further garages before following the others to W.North near Leeds. Nothing further is documented for these three vehicles and it must therefore be presumed that they were scrapped. (N.Rayfield)

GS42 was transferred from Dorking to Garston in February 1955 and stands within the roadway of its new residence. It could hardly have been envisaged at this stage that seventeen years later in the ownership of London Country Bus Services this bus would help perform the last rites of the GS on Route 336A at this same garage. Routes 361 and 309 had previously been operated by Mann Egerton bodied 15T13s until three GSs were allocated in May 1954. The 361 route shuttled between Rickmansworth and Chorleywood and the garage working shown on this blind was as long if not longer than the normal route. (Roy Marshall)

On delivery to the LTE in October 1952, green liveried RLH22 was put into service from Godstone garage. In February 1955 the first movement of Country Area liveried examples to the Central Area took place. RLH21/22/23 moved to Hornchurch garage to work on Route 248 together with red RLH76 replacing single deck TD class vehicles which had proved too small for the increasingly busy route which operated between Hall Lane, Upminster and Cranham. RLH22 and 23 received red livery later in the year but the former is seen here at Upminster Station before this repaint took place. (A.B.Cross)

APPENDIX I

London Transport Central and Country Area Bus Garages

A	Sutton	K	Kingston
AB	Twickenham	L	Loughton
AC	Willesden	LH*	Leatherhead
AD	Palmers Green	LS*	Luton
AE	Hendon	M	Mortlake
AF	Chelverton Road, Putney	MA*	Amersham
AK	Streatham	MH	Muswell Hill
AL	Merton	N	Norwood
AM	Plumstead	NB	Norbiton
AP	Seven Kings	NF*	Northfleet
AR	Tottenham	NS	North Street, Romford
AV	Hounslow	NX	New Cross
AW	Abbey Wood	ON	Alperton
B	Battersea	P	Old Kent Road
BK	Barking	PB	Potters Bar
BN	Brixton	PM	Peckham
C	Athol Street, Poplar	Q	Camberwell
CA	Clapham	R	Riverside
CF	Chalk Farm	RD	Hornchurch
CL	Clay Hall	RE*	London Road, Romford
CM*	Chelsham	RG*	Reigate
CS	Chiswick (non-operational)	RL	Rye Lane
CY*	Crawley	S	Shepherds Bush
D	Dalston	SA*	St.Albans
DG*	Dunton Green	SJ*	Swanley Junction
DS*	Dorking	SP	Sidcup
DT*	Dartford	ST*	Staines
E	Enfield	SV*	Stevenage
ED	Elmers End	SW	Stockwell
EG*	East Grinstead	T	Leyton
EP*	Epping	TB	Bromley
EW	Edgware	TC	Croydon
F	Putney Bridge	TG*	Tring
G	Forest Gate	TH	Thornton Heath
GD*	Godstone	TL	Catford
GF*	Guildford	TW*	Tunbridge Wells
GM	Gillingham Street, Victoria	U	Upton Park
GR*	Garston	UX	Uxbridge
GY*	Grays	V	Turnham Green
H	Hackney	W	Cricklewood
HD	Harrow Weald	WA*	Watford High Street
HE*	High Wycombe	WD	Wandsworth
HF*	Hatfield	WG	West Green
HG*	Hertford	WL	Walworth
HH*	Two Waters, Hemel Hempstead	WR*	Windsor
HN*	Hitchin	WY*	Addlestone
HW	Southall	X	Middle Row
J	Holloway	-	Aldenham (non-operational)

* indicates a Country Area garage.

A relatively quiet year with regard to garages, no new ones were brought into use and none were found to be surplus to requirements. The official opening of Aldenham Works took place in October. Engines, gearboxes, axles and electrical items were dealt with at Chiswick while the chassis and bodies were dealt with at Aldenham using returned major components from Chiswick. At full capacity Aldenham could deal with 56 vehicles per week.

APPENDIX II

Many more correspondents have communicated since the last published book in this series and I thank the following for their interest and helpful comments and information: James H.Aston, Terence Atkins, E.S.Baker, Nicholas Bennett, John C.Cese, Dr.A.Gilks, Philip Groves, Colin Lawrence, Nicholas Rothon, Peter Smith, Brian Speller, G.F.Stark, James Stirling of 'Allsorts', Croxley Green and Victor A.Wheal. The following distillation of their wisdom is published to enhance the previous books in this series.

1946 BOOK

Page 59   Ex-NS429 is parked in Warner Road, Camberwell; the photographer standing in the entrance to Camberwell garage to take this view with the Peabody Estate as a background.

Page 76   C61 is indeed in Westerham and showing the correct destination but using a display intended for another route. It should be showing 485. The 465 operated between Holland and Edenbridge paralleling the 485 between Crockham Hill and Edenbridge.

Page 110   The location of the lower photograph is at the final bus stop at Honor Oak on Route 63. The bus will now reverse across the road into a small turning beside the Forest Hill Tavern before pulling forward on to the stand – an impossible manouevre nowadays.

Page 115   The bottom picture of ST988 is taken in Merton Road, Southfields outside what was then Merton Road School, now renamed Riversdale School.

Page 129   The lower picture of LT911 is not as captioned at Honor Oak but rather at the bombed King's Arms, Peckham Rye. The point is made that it is unusual for a crew change to be made on the 'up' trip as appears to be happening here. The normal procedure being on the 'down' journey as captioned in the top picture on page 121.

Page 139   The line of buses in Gordon Road, Kingston is the result of a strike, of which there were quite a few in the 1950s.

Page 146   Several people have assisted with information on the decrepit vehicle at Wanstead Flats. It now seems positive that this is former Thomas Tilling 'O' 139 which was registered XR739.

1948 BOOK

Page 60   The top picture shows G159 travelling along Ripple Road, Barking just south of 'Blakes Corner'.

Page 86   G316 is standing in Linton Road, Barking at the stand for 'Blakes Corner'. Note the working is one of the journeys to Dagenham, Church Elm which is a bifurcation off the main 87 route at the 'Chequers', Dagenham, a one time feature of Saturday afternoon working.

Page 129   The extension of Route 96 from Wanstead (The George) to The Red House public house opposite the site of Redbridge Station took place on 11th May 1932. On the wartime restricted blinds both the terminus at The George used by Routes 40 and 101 and that at The Red House used by 96 were simply described as 'Wanstead'. When the Central Line extension was opened in December 1947 The Red House terminus was renamed 'Redbridge Station' but it was the same place.

1950 BOOK

Page 21   LT737 is confirmed as standing in High Street South at East Ham opposite the fire station. It is suggested that it is either being used as an engineer's bus on a mission of mercy to a stricken vehicle on Route 101 or on a London Transport contract to transport school children to the East Ham Baths which were also across the road in Nelson Street. LTs were noted on this duty in January 1950.

Page 93   The top picture was taken at the Ferndale Street stand, Cyprus, Royal Albert Dock.

Page 118   Passengers are boarding G31 in Barking Road, Canning Town at the eastbound bus stop on the west side of the junction with Hermit Road.

1952 BOOK

Page 32   G311 has stopped in East Ham High Street South just north of the By-pass, rather than in East Ham Manor Way which started at the south side of the By-pass.

Page 63   In the top picture RTL1050 is standing at the Stepney East Station terminus.

Page 73   SRT114 is at the Green Man terminus in Bush Road, Leytonstone. Careful inspection of the road surface reveals that this length by the bus stop is in fact metal surfaced, which was originally laid down in 1932.

1954 BOOK

Page 64   The top picture shows RTL642 standing outside Mr.Loft's shop in Turnpike Lane, situated at the 41 bus stop for Turnpike Lane Station just before the road widened out in front of the 'Wellington' public house and not in West Green Road as captioned.

Page 89   RT1515 is approaching the Ilford Broadway traffic signals at the top of Ilford Hill.

1955 BOOK

Page 34   The exact location of the top picture is Stephendale Road which leads off the east side of Wandsworth Bridge Road.

Page 129   Initially Route 720A diverged from the main 720 route at Old Harlow, turning up First Avenue to terminate at The Stow. The diversion at Potter Street to run via Brays Grove to the Town Centre was not introduced until 11th July 1956.